W9-DID-263

WAR IN THE PACIFIC

The most important, explosive, and strategic battles of World War Two took place in the Pacific arena, as the seemingly invincible Japanese sought to expand their notorious empire. Now this astonishing era comes to life in a breathtakingly authentic new series by noted historian Edwin P. Hoyt that places the reader in the heart of the earth-shattering conflict—a dramatic, detailed chronicle of military brilliance and extraordinary human courage on the bloody battlefields of land and sea.

VOLUME
III

SOUTH PACIFIC

J. G. BERLENDIS
502 Powell St.
Bisbee, AZ. 85603

Other Avon Books in the
WAR IN THE PACIFIC *series by*
Edwin P. Hoyt

VOLUME I: TRIUMPH OF JAPAN
VOLUME II: STIRRINGS

Coming Soon

PEARL HARBOR

and don't miss the start
of the exciting new
WAR IN EUROPE *series by*
Edwin P. Hoyt

VOLUME I: BLITZKRIEG

Avon Books are available at special quantity discounts for bulk purchases for sales promotions, premiums, fund raising or educational use. Special books, or book excerpts, can also be created to fit specific needs.

For details write or telephone the office of the Director of Special Markets, Avon Books, Dept. FP, 1350 Avenue of the Americas, New York, New York 10019, 212-261-6800.

WAR IN THE PACIFIC

VOLUME III

SOUTH PACIFIC

EDWIN P. HOYT

AVON BOOKS ◆ NEW YORK

If you purchased this book without a cover, you should be aware that this book is stolen property. It was reported as "unsold and destroyed" to the publisher, and neither the author nor the publisher has received any payment for this "stripped book."

WAR IN THE PACIFIC, VOLUME III: SOUTH PACIFIC is an original publication of Avon Books. This work has never before appeared in book form.

AVON BOOKS
A division of
The Hearst Corporation
1350 Avenue of the Americas
New York, New York 10019

Copyright © 1991 by Edwin P. Hoyt
Published by arrangement with the author
Library of Congress Catalog Card Number: 91-91785
ISBN: 0-380-76158-0

All rights reserved, which includes the right to reproduce this book or portions thereof in any form whatsoever except as provided by the U.S. Copyright Law. For information address Avon Books.

First Avon Books Printing: August 1991

AVON TRADEMARK REG. U.S. PAT. OFF. AND IN OTHER COUNTRIES, MARCA REGISTRADA, HECHO EN U.S.A.

Printed in the U.S.A.

RA   10   9   8   7   6   5   4   3   2   1

CONTENTS

PREFACE

On August 7, 1942, the American First Marine Division and supporting troops landed on Guadalcanal and Tulagi islands in the Solomons group. Their mission was to forestall Japanese utilization of a seaplane base on Tulagi and a newly constructed airfield on Guadalcanal that was designed to cut the American lifeline to Australia, where General Douglas MacArthur was preparing an offensive against the until-now victorious Japanese. This first Allied amphibious landing of the Pacific war was hurriedly conceived. Fortunately, the Japanese were totally surprised and the only vigorous land defense was conducted in the Tulagi area, where the Japanese were quickly overwhelmed by superior forces.

Vice Admiral Frank Jack Fletcher, commander of the three aircraft carriers supporting the landing, was very nervous about the whole operation and worried lest he lose one of the three precious carriers under his command. Therefore he announced on the eve of the landings that they would have forty-eight hours of carrier air support—no more. Rear Admiral Richmond Kelly Turner, commander of the amphibious forces, protested that no other air support was available for the ships and the 16,000 men ashore in the Solomons, but to no avail. Admiral Fletcher did not even wait the forty-eight hours, but began moving his ships south on the evening of August 8, leaving the marines ashore and at the mercy of superior Japanese naval and air forces.

1

CHAPTER ONE

The First Disaster

The decision had been made on July 26, 1942, eleven days before the marine landings on Guadalcanal. At a conference aboard the Guadalcanal expedition flagship, the carrier *Saratoga*, Vice Admiral Frank Jack Fletcher had announced after two days that he was withdrawing air support from the expedition to protect his three aircraft carriers.

Rear Admiral Richmond Kelly Turner had objected, at first quietly, then with growing heat, until the conference became a shouting match between Fletcher and Turner. The major objection to the withdrawal was that it would place the marines at the mercy of Japanese air and sea power. Admiral Fletcher ignored that claim, although it was repeated several times. In the course of the argument it became apparent to those at the conference that Fletcher was opposed to the whole Guadalcanal operation, which had been specifically ordered by Admiral Ernest J. King, the chief of the American navy.

There was no recourse to Admiral Fletcher's decision, because he was the senior officer present. Actually, Vice Admiral Robert Ghormley had been ordered by Admiral Chester W. Nimitz, commander of the Pacific Fleet, to take personal command of the Guadalcanal operation. But Ghormley, who also objected to the landings as ill-timed and ill-planned, had not attended this vital meeting, but had remained at his headquarters at Auckland, New Zealand, more than a thousand miles from the scene of the action.

Because the landings completely surprised the Japanese, they were successful, albeit disorganized and confused. At one point the commander of the landing boats landed on Guadalcanal and found supplies piling up on the beaches. About twenty men were unloading boats, while another fifty men had gone swimming! By nightfall there were a hundred landed boats on the beach, not yet unloaded, and fifty boats lying offshore, waiting for space to land.

There were two high-level air raids on the area on August 7, but they did minimal damage. The big problem was confusion, and it continued. The night of August 7 virtually nothing was done. On the morning of August 8 work began again to get the nineteen transports and cargo ships unloaded, but again, confusion reigned, made more serious by an air raid alert at 10:40 that morning. Still, in twenty-six hours of actual unloading most of the supplies of the transports were gotten out of the holds and onto the beaches by late afternoon on August 8.

The afternoon of August 7, Japanese dive-bombers conducted one of two air raids, and one of them bombed the destroyer *Mugford*. When Admiral Fletcher heard that, he grew even more nervous, because he had been under criticism for losing two carriers already (the *Lexington* at the Battle of the Coral Sea, and the *Yorktown* at the Battle of Midway*).

Where had the Japanese dive-bombers come from? Fletcher was worried that they came from Japanese carriers, for he knew that four major Japanese carriers were available at this time and might be in the South Pacific. Rear Admiral Leigh Noyes, commander of the air support group, tried to reassure Fletcher that the dive-bombers came from the Japanese Twenty-fifth Air Flotilla based at Rabaul, but Fletcher was not convinced. His concerns grew, because on the day before the invasion, General MacArthur's command had reported (erroneously) sighting a carrier to the west of the invasion force.

Admiral Noyes was also nervous, and on August 8, when coast watchers reported forty large twin-engined planes

*See Volume II of this series.

heading south from Rabaul, he refused to divert planes from the combat air patrol to protect the amphibious forces. So, before ten o'clock that morning, it was known that the Japanese had sent a large force of torpedo bombers against Turner's ships, and nothing was being done about it.

The attack came in and was repulsed by heavy antiaircraft fire from the ships. It was reported to Fletcher, but he did not believe the planes were carrying torpedoes! (One torpedo missed the stern of Admiral Turner's command ship, the *McCawley*, by forty feet.) The Japanese torpedoed the destroyer *Jarvis*, which was sunk next day by other Japanese planes. When Fletcher was assured that these really were torpedo planes, he got the wind up, and worried all the next day.

One of Fletcher's anxieties concerned the high level of fighter plane losses during the two days of the landings. The losses were largely operational, which meant accidents, not enemy action. He, like many another American, knew that the Japanese Zero fighter was superior to the American fighters, and that worried him. He was very much afraid of Japanese torpedo planes, which were also superior to the American equivalent of that day. So he decided that the original decision to withdraw and protect the carrier force had been correct, and at six o'clock on the evening of August 8, sent a message to Admiral Ghormley, his chief in the South Pacific, recommending withdrawal of the carriers toward the south, leaving the marines and Guadalcanal and Admiral Turner's ships without any air support.

And then, without waiting for a reply to his message, Admiral Fletcher turned and headed south. He was about 120 miles from Savo Island. When he announced the withdrawal and began to move, many officers of the carrier force were dismayed. They had read messages that indicated the Japanese were sending a naval force south, and although the messages were very vague, they knew something was going to happen.

Admiral Turner received a copy of that message and hoped that Ghormley would turn Fletcher down. But Ghormley had not liked the Guadalcanal operation from the outset, and he, too, was worried about risking carriers in what he considered to be an ill-conceived and premature plan to fight back against the Japanese.

The afternoon of August 8, Admiral Turner had very little information, although he did know that an enemy force was heading his way. But the reports were still vague and mentioned seaplane tenders. The various Allied commanders were expecting air attack and the establishment of new seaplane bases around Guadalcanal to carry it out. And they were really not getting any information from the various air commands that were supposed to be carrying out air searches.

But the air searches late on August 8 were not successful and were hampered by bad weather. So the hours went by and Admiral Turner did not receive any new information. Admiral Fletcher was supposed to make a late-afternoon air search north of Guadalcanal, but he was preoccupied with retiring at high speed, so he did not. At this point, Admiral Turner, who was entrusted with the responsibility of protecting the marines on Guadalcanal and Tulagi, now that he had delivered them, called Rear Admiral V.A.C. Crutchley of the Australian navy, and the cruiser commander of the invasion, to consult. Crutchley arrived at Lunga Roads at 10:30 that night for a conference with Turner and General Alexander Vandegrift.

In view of Fletcher's known insistence on retiring, Admiral Turner knew his chances were that he would not have air support, so he asked Crutchley if he thought he could stick out the next few days without air support. Inherent in this question was both admirals' knowledge of the capability of the Japanese Twenty-fifth Air Flotilla at Rabaul, which had already been attacking them, and had sunk the destroyer *Jarvis* and the transport *George F. Elliott* during the landing phase.

At the meeting Crutchley and Turner agreed on the night disposition of the Allied cruisers forces to protect the transports off Guadalcanal. Crutchley split the forces into four, one a southern force which he commanded. This consisted of the cruisers *Australia*, *Canberra*, and *Chicago*, together with the destroyers *Bagley* and *Patterson*. They began to patrol from Savo Island to Cape Esperance, on the northern tip of Guadalcanal to the south.

The second force, the northern, would block the entrance to the narrow sea area known as the Slot, between Savo and Florida islands. This consisted of the cruisers *Vincennes, Astoria,* and *Quincy* and the destroyers *Helm* and *Wilson.*

The two destroyers that made up the third force, the *Blue* and the *Ralph Talbot,* were assigned to patrol west of Savo Island. The area east of Lunga Point was to be patrolled by the fourth force, the light cruisers *San Juan* and *Hobart* and the destroyers *Monssen* and *Buchanan.*

When these dispositions were made, Admiral Crutchley went back to his flagship and the Guadalcanal force prepared to settle in for the night, with the transports unloading until morning. General Vandegrift agreed that the transports had best head out then, although he was loath to do so. He now had 18,000 marines on shore, with the prospect of inadequate supply and no air or naval support.

There was no battle plan, because Admiral Turner and Crutchley had no reason to expect a battle before the next day, when, hopefully, the transports would have retired to safety. Crutchley asked what Turner expected. Turner replied that he expected the Japanese to establish a seaplane base at Rekata Bay, and then, next day, to launch seaplanes carrying torpedos. He told Crutchley that he had asked Rear Admiral John S. McCain, commander of the land-based air force in the South Pacific, to bomb shipping in Rekata Bay the next morning. That might forestall the enemy attack Turner expected.

What about a surface raid by the Japanese?

It was a possibility, Turner agreed, but there were no indications of a very strong force coming from anywhere, and the Allied ship disposition seemed adequate to meet what might threaten. That was what Admiral Turner believed, based on the information available to him.

But on August 7, shortly after the news of the invasion was radioed from Tulagi, the Japanese had begun to react to the Guadalcanal landings, even though they did not really understand the nature or the extent of the attack. They did know that a large number of ships were standing off Guadalcanal and off Florida Island, which is behind little Tulagi. This was enough for Vice Admiral Gunichi Mikawa, commander of the Japanese Eighth Fleet at Rabaul. He decided to act.

The force was readily available, and already in motion. Five heavy Japanese cruisers had just left Kavieng, New Guinea, that morning. Mikawa called them to Rabaul, and they arrived off the port in the middle of the afternoon of August 7. The cruiser *Chokai* and the destroyer *Yunagi* went into Simpson Harbor to report, and the remainder of the force moved toward St. George Channel at the end of New Britain to await them.

Mikawa had a problem: a shortage of destroyers. He had cruisers, but only one destroyer was available because the army's demand for supply convoys was so great. So he had to be content with that single destroyer, and thus had no real antisubmarine screen. Admiral Mikawa went aboard the *Chokai* and led the force out of Rabaul the evening of August 7, taking also the light cruisers *Tenryu* and *Yubari*. By evening, seven cruisers were on the way to oppose the Americans at Guadalcanal.

Meanwhile, the MacArthur command was too new, and the whole Allied defensive organization too disorganized to function very efficiently. Most of the air scouting activity was accomplished by Australian Hudson bombers and American B-17s, and they did not immediately realize the the naval forces' need for immediate information about ship sighting. Therefore, although B-17s spotted the Japanese ships in St. George's Channel on the afternoon of August 7, it was after eleven P.M. when the MacArthur command sent a message to the South Pacific command about sighting six unidentified ships in St. George's Channel. Later that night the cruiser force was spotted by the U.S. submarine *S-38* in St. George's Channel, coming so close to the submarine that it had no chance to fire torpedoes and was rocked by the wash from the ships as they moved past. Lieutenant Commander H. G. Munson radioed a contact report of two destroyers and three larger ships moving southeast at high speed.

Admiral Mikawa ordered up the equivalent of a reinforced battalion of naval landing troops, loaded them on six transports, and dispatched them to Guadalcanal. He did not, of course, know that this was a major invasion and that by the end of the first day, 11,000 marines were ashore in the Solomons.

In midmorning on August 8 a Hudson bomber of the Australian air force sighted the cruiser force and began to follow it. The Japanese changed course to deceive the Allied plane, and seemed to be milling about in the strait that lies between Bougainville and Choiseul. Another Australian search plane also sighted the group and gave a slightly different report. General MacArthur's headquarters thus received two reports about several ships heading southeast. They knew how many were destroyers and how many were cruisers, at least five ships were identified.

That morning Admiral Mikawa learned more about his enemies, two floatplanes sent off from the cruisers returned to report many ships in the water around Tulagi and Guadalcanal. So Admiral Mikawa headed south at 24 knots through Bougainville Strait and into New Georgia Sound south of Choiseul. By this time it was four o'clock on the afternoon of August 8.

Admiral Mikawa decided to make a stealthy night attack because he knew that the American sailors and aviators were not trained for night action while, because of the months of night training ordered by Admiral Yamamoto, the Japanese were very skillful at night fighting.

As the Japanese force hurried toward Guadalcanal, Admiral Mikawa issued his battle plan by blinker to every ship in his force: "On the rush in we will go from south of Savo Island and torpedo the enemy main force in front of the Guadalcanal anchorage, after which we will turn toward the Tulagi forward area to shell and torpedo the enemy. We will then withdraw north of Savo Island."

Two seaplanes from the cruisers *Chokai* and *Aoba* flew off shortly after four o'clock that afternoon for a final check on the whereabouts of the Allied ships. So, as darkness closed down on the Guadalcanal area, the Japanese knew where their enemy was, while the Americans and Australians did not know where the Japanese were, or that they were actually closing in.

That night the Japanese reinforcing troops from Rabaul were reaching a point west of Cape St. George at the southwest corner of New Britain Island when the *S-38*, one of the submarines of the old Asiatic Fleet, spotted the transport *Meiyo Maru* with an escorting destroyer. Lieutenant Commander Munson took the submarine down and fired two torpedoes. They both connected and the *Meiyo Maru* sank, with the loss of many of the reinforcing troops. This loss persuaded Admiral Mikawa that before he could reinforce the southern Solomons he had to be sure of sea supremacy, so he called back the expeditionary force, and proceeded with his naval force instead.

Four allied forces were patrolling the sea area that led to Guadalcanal that night, as the Japanese steamed down on them at 26 knots. Off the Guadalcanal shore the marines were unloading as fast as they could to get supplies ashore before dawn.

At 11:30 that night heavy rain began to fall around Savo Island, obscuring the view of the northern and southern Allied cruiser forces patrolling there. From above the Allied sailors could hear the sounds of aircraft—these were two more scout planes launched from Admiral Mikawa's cruisers to check the dispositions of the Allied ships.

The watch of the destroyer *Ralph Talbot* identified one of the planes as a Japanese cruiser-type seaplane and issued the warning. But nobody aboard Admiral Turner's flagship was listening—even though he was only twenty miles away. Other ship watches saw one or the other of the planes but disregarded them, believing they were friendly because they were running their lights. So the planes flew overhead, reporting to Admiral Mikawa the dispositions, courses, and speeds of the Allied ships below, and nobody bothered them. Midnight came and all was quiet around Guadalcanal except for the droning of the planes overhead. A junior officer aboard the American cruiser *Quincy* said that they must be enemy planes, but he was hooted down as hysterical and ignored.

On the bridge of the *Chokai*, Japanese Admiral Mikawa received the reports of his planes. He was particularly interested in the news that an Allied transport was burning off Guadalcanal. It would be a beacon to his ships as they swooped down on the landing place. That was the objective, the fat transports, not the protective Allied naval force.

Admiral Mikawa had his ships strung out in a long line,

with intervals of three-quarters of a mile in between. First came the flagship *Chokai*, then the heavy cruisers *Aoba*, *Kako*, *Kinugasa*, and *Furutaka*, then the light cruisers *Tenryu* and *Yubari*, and the single destroyer *Yunagi*. They were to steam into Lunga Roads, attack the transports off Guadalcanal, then hit those off Tulagi and turn and run for the north, to get beyond the range of carrier planes by daylight.

Just before one A.M., the lookouts aboard *Chokai* sighted the destroyer *Blue* on their starboard bow, heading southwest. The gunners were prepared to shoot, but the watch on *Blue* did not see a thing, and so she passed safely by. Mikawa moved to enter the sound between Savo Island and Cape Esperance and kept Savo Island on the port side. At 1:34, Mikawa ordered his ships to attack as soon as possible—they were to fire torpedoes. In quick order they passed three Allied destroyers, the *Jarvis*, *Patterson*, and *Bagley*. They fired torpedoes at the *Jarvis*, mistaking her for a cruiser, but they all missed.

But now the cruisers *Chicago* and *Canberra* were coming into sight, seven miles away. The Japanese rushed to attack, and then the American destroyer *Patterson* spotted them and raised the alarm. At almost the same moment the Japanese cruiser seaplanes dropped flares over the transports at Lunga Roads, which silhouetted the cruisers *Chicago* and *Canberra*, only three miles from the Japanese flagship *Chokai*. The *Chokai*, *Aoba*, and *Furutaka* had already fired torpedoes and now they fired their guns.

Two torpedoes smashed into the *Canberra*, and shells began hitting her. Her crew managed to fire two torpedoes and a few shots, but she was swiftly struck by twenty-four shells, and in five minutes was wrecked, and her captain and gunnery officer dead.

The *Patterson* was hit by one shell, and her crew was so startled they did not hear an order to fire torpedoes. The destroyer *Bagley*, near the Japanese, was not fired on because the enemy cruisers were busy with bigger game. Having disposed of the *Canberra*, they turned to the *Chicago* and sent a torpedo into her, knocking off part of the bow. The *Chicago* gunners saw something and began firing. That something was the Japanese destroyer *Yunagi*. The cruiser fired several shells at her, but the destroyer disappeared in the murk.

The Allied vessels still had their guns trained fore and aft, an indication of their unreadiness for combat. That was the basic Allied difficulty—mostly American—that night: they were surprised by many phenomena because they had not yet accommodated themselves to war. The assumptions that aircraft overhead would be friendly because they were showing lights was an indication of the American naivete.

The Japanese force split into two segments, and Admiral Mikawa turned north toward three more Allied cruisers, the *Vincennes*, *Quincy*, and *Astoria*, and the destroyers *Helm* and *Wilson*. At 1:48 A.M. the *Chokai* fired four torpedoes. A few seconds later the floatplane flares illuminated the area, and the *Astoria* began firing. The *Astoria*'s captain, awakened from sleep in his cabin, thought his gunners were firing on their own ships and ordered them to stop. So they did. By the time they started again, the gunners of the *Chokai* had the range and set the *Astoria* afire, which gave the Japanese gunners an aiming point. Shells began to strike home, and soon the *Astoria* was blazing, her speed down to seven knots, and her black gang trying to get out of the inferno below. She fired twelve salvos and one hit a forward turret on the *Chokai*.

The *Aoba* came up on the *Quincy* and snapped on her searchlights, illuminating the American cruiser. Her captain saw ships, but thought they were Allied vessels and prevented his gunners from firing. Soon she was caught in a crossfire between the two Japanese groups of ships and fires illuminated her brightly. A torpedo hit the side of the No. 4 fireroom. The *Quincy* got in a lick or two and two of her shells struck the *Chokai*, wiping out the Admiral's chart room. But she took a beating. A shell just about cleared the bridge, killing the captain, and in moments the *Quincy* was a wreck of a ship. At 2:35 she capsized.

By 1:50 A.M. the *Vincennes* was also under fire from the Japanese. She was firing, and with her second salvo she hit the *Kinugasa*. But at that moment, several shells from the Japanese cruisers struck the *Vincennes* and she, too, began to blaze. The *Vincennes* was hit by three torpedoes from the *Chokai*, blowing out her insides. Just after two A.M.

another torpedo struck in the No. 1 fireroom and killed the crew. The ship went dead in the water, but the Japanese continued to shoot. By 2:15 she was burning and helpless and the Japanese had moved on.

As all this sound and fury continued, the transports stopped unloading and got under way at Guadalcanal and Tulagi. At 2:40 A.M. all was quiet. Admiral Mikawa's ships had turned north and were running back toward Japanese waters, and the Allies were left to pick up the pieces. Admiral Turner prepared to take his transports and retire from the area.

So the battle of Savo Island was over. The Allies had lost the cruisers *Quincy*, *Canberra*, *Vincennes*, and *Astoria*, and the *Chicago* had been badly damaged. The Japanese had lost no ships and had suffered relatively little damage. Fifty-eight Japanese sailors had been killed and about fifty wounded—a tiny price to pay for four American cruisers. Concerned about possible Allied air retaliation, Admiral Mikawa ordered speed increase to 30 knots as the Japanese ran north.

There was to be no retaliation. True, Admiral Fletcher was having some second thoughts about his decision to abandon Guadalcanal. The carrier force had been steaming along all evening, actually having been on the run for nearly twelve hours. It had nearly cleared San Cristobal Island, southwest of Guadalcanal, at one A.M. on August 9, when Admiral Fletcher had some misgivings and turned back toward Guadalcanal. He had not gotten the message he expected from Admiral Ghormley, concurring in his decision to abandon the transports and the marines, and was obviously worried about his most unmilitary posture. He also knew that Admiral Mikawa was not quite correct in his assumption that the Americans knew nothing about night fighting. The carrier *Wasp* had been trained as a night carrier, which meant her pilots would have been able to attack the Japanese cruiser force if they had been in the Guadalcanal area.

At three A.M. came a report of a surface action near Guadalcanal. Captain Forrest Sherman of the *Wasp* requested permission from Rear Admiral Noyes, who was riding in the *Wasp*, to hurry northwest and attack the Japanese force. But that permission was refused by Noyes, who would not even forward the request to Admiral Fletcher. At about this time Fletcher got the message he wanted from Admiral Ghormley, that it was all right to abandon Guadalcanal, and he turned the force again, heading south, away from the action.

At Guadalcanal, the stink of defeat acrid in his nostrils, Admiral Turner stopped the retreat and ordered the transports to resume unloading. The Japanese might return. They most assuredly would send an air strike the next day. But the transports had to be unloaded before they moved, or the men on Guadalcanal would soon be desperate for supply. By mid-afternoon on August 9 the marines had a thirty-seven-day supply of food and a minimal supply of ammunition. That afternoon the transports left for Noumea in two groups.

Admiral Mikawa had won a signal victory, for which he was congratulated by Admiral Yamamoto (who was critical, however, of the fact that Mikawa had not come back and sunk the transports). The only marring factor was the sinking that next day of the cruiser *Kako* by the American submarine *S-44* off Kavieng. But there was no retaliatory air attack from the Americans. Mikawa had expected one and could not quite understand why it did not come. Neither could Admiral Nimitz and Admiral King.

An investigation into the debacle was begun by Admiral Arthur J. Hepburn. It was wartime, and an extremely awkward moment to be washing the navy's dirty linen in public. So the causes of the disaster were muffled. But in very short order, Vice Admiral Frank Jack Fletcher was removed from his command and so was Rear Admiral Leigh Noyes. Admiral King wanted fighting leaders in charge of naval action, men who would risk ships to win victories.

So, on August 9, 1942, the marines settled down on Guadalcanal without air support, with inadequate sea support, to see what the Japanese would throw at them.

CHAPTER TWO

After the Nightmare

No one in Washington had anticipated that, forty-eight hours after the First Marine Division and attached troops were landed on Guadalcanal, they would be abandoned without either air or sea cover. But after the withdrawal of Admiral Fletcher's carrier fleet and the destruction of four cruisers and a destroyer, the remaining Allied sea force was hardly adequate for defense. So, on the afternoon of August 9, the combat ships escorted the transports south, out of danger, and the marines were alone.

This move left General Alexander Vandegrift facing the whole problem of defense, but with not much to work with. There had not been time to set up antiaircraft guns or heavy artillery, so the largest pieces were some 75-mm self-propelled guns and a captured Japanese 3-inch gun. The rest were 37-mm antitank guns and .50-calibre machine-guns. To guard against the Japanese reinforcement of Guadalcanal which he expected, General Vandegrift set up a five-mile defense perimeter, which ran from the Tenaru River to Kukum. Other marines were put to work setting up the 90-mm antiaircraft guns around the airfield, and still others, to getting the airfield ready for operations.

On August 7, when the first news of the marine landings reached Rabaul, the initial reaction of the Japanese was not very pronounced. In Tokyo, Imperial General Headquarters estimated that there were only about 2000 American troops involved, and that it was really a raid, or a reconnaissance in force, which could be handled without any particular problems. The chief of the naval general staff went to Nikko, one of Emperor Hirohito's summer villas, to inform the emperor of the fact, and to reassure him that there was no cause for alarm.

At Rabaul, the Japanese Twenty-fifth Air Flotilla, which was the navy unit charged with defense of the area, sent fifty-one planes against the attackers. Thirty of them did not return, which was disconcerting, but not alarming. Guadalcanal was a long way from Rabaul, and many planes were lost due to operational accidents or to ditching on the way home from the action. That, of course, was the reason the navy had built the airfield on Guadalcanal, to give a forward access base.

Because under the Japanese system of command division the navy was responsible for the sea and air protection of such island territories as the Solomons and New Guinea, the army general staff had no detailed knowledge of navy operations in the area. General Gen Sugiyama, the army chief of staff, had only the most rudimentary knowledge of the whole area. Colonel Takushiro Hattori, deputy chief of the Operations Division, learned on August 7 of the existence of the new airfield. Under the Japanese system there was no need for him to know, for the airfield would be used by the navy to attack the Australian air routes.

In Tokyo, then, the American Guadalcanal operation was regarded as a gnat's bite. But it was agreed that the American gnat had to be eliminated before the war could proceed in a purposeful fashion. General Hideki Tojo, the prime minister, took a more serious view of the landings. He regarded them as a threat, and ordered General Sugiyama to take over responsibility for the recapture of Guadalcanal from the navy, with whom it rested. Admiral Osami Nagano, the navy chief of staff, having reassured the emperor, sent a message to Admiral Isoroku Yamamoto, chief of the Imperial Combined Fleet, to do something. Yamamoto sent Vice Admiral Nishizo Tsukahara, commander of the Eleventh Air Fleet at Saipan (a land-based naval air force), to proceed to Rabaul and take command of the Southeast Area

Force. The swift recapture of Guadalcanal was made a first priority by the navy.

On Guadalcanal, the fighting marines proceeded slowly about their tasks, although they had not met opposition as had the marines attacking the Florida Island complex. The First Marines dawdled on the way to their objective, Grassy Knoll. The Fifth Marines reached their objective, the east bank of Alligator Creek, before nightfall on D-Day.

On the second day, August 8, the objectives were changed, the First Marines were instructed to surround the airfield and the Fifth Marines, to push on to Kukum. The Eleventh Marines (the artillery) moved to the airfield and found it deserted. By the end of August 8 the airfield was occupied.

On Sunday, August 9, General Vandegrift started early to pull his defenses together, not knowing the details of the disastrous Battle of Savo Island, but knowing that some sort of debacle had occurred. He set in motion plans to organize the defenses against an attack from the sea, to move the unloaded supplies to dispersal dumps inland; and to get the airfield, which was named Henderson Field in honor of a pilot killed at Midway, ready for action.

By evening of August 9, a defensive cordon stretched out from the Tenaru River to Lunga and then to a point a half-mile southwest of Kukum, armed with 37-mm and .50-calibre machine guns. The 90-mm antiaircraft guns were in place near the airfield. The half-tracks with the 75-mm guns were ready, and so were 75-mm pack howitzers. But there were big problems. The defeat of the naval forces and the flight of the transports had left a lot of holes. Take barbed wire. There were only eighteen spools of barbed wire on the island. All the rest of it was in the holds of the ships going back to Noumea. The ships had also carried away all the sandbags and all the digging tools. There were no anti-personnel mines for defense. But there was captured Japanese equipment. Four tractors, six road oilers, two gasoline locomotives, and a number of cars and trucks had been captured when the Japanese fled. So this equipment could be used to complete the airfield.

Marines began work on the airfield. Marines carried supplies to the dumps. Marines went on patrol, and one patrol reached the Matanikau River, a mile and a half west of Kukum, where it came under Japanese fire. An officer was killed and several enlisted men were wounded. The next day a platoon-sized patrol also encountered the enemy here, and the marines discovered that the Japanese survivors had concentrated in this area of Guadalcanal.

The marines captured a Japanese naval warrant officer, who, under interrogation, indicated that the Japanese were there. Colonel Frank B. Goettge, the division intelligence officer, supervised the interrogation. He had also heard that the Japanese might be persuaded to surrender. Someone on that patrol had seen a white flag. The Japanese captive indicated that the troops were hungry, deprived of supplies that had been abandoned in the Kukum area. Colonel Goettge proposed to lead a reconnaissance party on an amphibious landing west of the Matanikau. General Vandegrift was not enthusiastic, but he gave permission. Led by Colonel Goettge, the party was ambushed west of the Matanikau, and only three men survived. The white flag they discovered, was the regular Japanese Rising Sun flag, whose red center had been concealed earlier.

So, at the cost of the life of the division intelligence officer and a number of others, the marines learned something they ought to have known from the fighting on Tulagi: the Japanese code, Bushido, forbade their surrender. On Tulagi the Japanese had at last been driven into caves, and had fought there to the end. A number of marines had been killed or wounded in attacking the caves, and the solution had finally been to seal up the caves. Thus, in this first week of battle in which the Americans were on the offensive, they learned that the Japanese never gave up. This was not true in absolutely every case, but the marines thereafter operated mostly on that principle, and the fighting on Guadalcanal and elsewhere in the Pacific assumed a tone of "no quarter."

On August 9, 10, and 11, the weather grounded the Japanese planes at Rabaul, so the marines enjoyed a respite from attack. The airfield was now usable, as was proved by Admiral McCain's aide, who landed a PBY amphibian on the strip, but work on the field continued, to make it ready for a marine air squadron that had been promised. Although American rations were so short that the men were limited to two meals a day, they pieced out with Japanese food and rice, of which there was a fair supply. So morale among the marines was good, and they expected that soon the army garrison force would arrive and the marines would be relieved.

Rabaul was also brimming over with optimism. The easy victory of Admiral Mikawa obscured the loss of more than half the air attack force of the first day, and the absence of the transports obscured the size of the American presence on Guadalcanal. From Tokyo came notes of optimism. The military attaché in Moscow had learned about the American invasion, and his report said American morale was low and that the mission of the troops was to destroy the airfield and withdraw.

In Tokyo, General Tojo decreed that the cleanup of Guadalcanal would be accomplished by the army, not the navy, and thus that the reinforcing force in the transports sent back by Admiral Mikawa would not sail again. General Sugiyama was to make the decision as to which army units would be employed. On orders from Tojo, Sugiyama and Admiral Nagano met and made a new agreement changing the areas of responsibility in the South Pacific. It had primarily been a navy show, but now the army would take responsibility for the land fighting. The army would capture Port Moresby, and the army would retake Guadalcanal and Tulagi. Lieutenant General Harukichi Hyukatake, commander of the Seventeenth Army, was sent to Rabaul to decide what to do. His intelligence seemed to reaffirm the report that there were about 2000 Americans on Guadalcanal and Tulagi.

Imperial Headquarters assigned the Thirty-fifth Infantry Brigade and two reinforced regiments to Hyukatake, though they were not at Rabaul, but scattered across the Pacific. The closest infantry unit that could help was the Twenty-eighth Infantry Regiment, commanded by Colonel Kiyanao Ichiki. That was a crack unit, which had been scheduled to make the assault on Midway and been carried in the ships on the expedition, but had been returned to Juan after the invasion was aborted and was now scheduled to go back to Japan.

On August 12, the vice chief of staff of the Japanese army suggested that it was not necessary to employ so many troops as a brigade and reinforced regiments to deal with the Americans. Since there were supposedly only 2000 Americans in the Solomons, Colonel Ichiki should be able to handle them without even employing all his regiment, just a detachment which could move quickly and economically. The effectiveness of the small, tight unit had become a matter of Japanese army doctrine and it was shored up by the remarkable performance of General Yamashita's troops in the assault on Malaya and Singapore, where he had defeated a much larger British force with deceptive ease. So the army brass decided that a detachment of perhaps 2500 men could do the job because they were obviously so superior to the enemy.

At this time the word "marine" meant nothing to the Japanese army command, which had shown an arrogant lack of respect for all the enemies they had defeated so easily in recent months. Most of them had quite forgotten an experience with the Russians at Nomonhon, for instance, where the Kwantung Army had assaulted the Soviets and lost more than a whole division of men to Marshal Zhukov's forces.

Some of the officers at Imperial General Headquarters objected to this overconfidence, but General Sugiyama refused to budge, and General Tojo would not push him. So the decision was made, and on August 13, Colonel Ichiki had his orders. He was then at Truk, where Operation KA would be launched.

Colonel Ichiki would take an advance unit of 900 men on six destroyers to Taivu Point, about twenty miles east of the American position. Meanwhile, a small naval landing force of 250 men would land near Kokumbona, in a feint maneuver. They would reconnoiter, assess the situation and, if possible, engage and destroy the enemy. If they could not recapture the airfield, they would wait for the arrival of the rest of the detachment, about 1500 troops, who were promised within a week.

Why all the hurry?

Because the Japanese were eager to get on with the capture of Port Moresby, and the air assault from Guadalcanal airfields was a major factor in that plan. The "victory disease" had permeated the army and the navy at Tokyo, with the military leaders firmly believing their own propaganda about the Japanese being unbeatable. There were some more level heads, and General Hyukatake's was one of them. If Imperial General Headquarters insisted on immediate action, let them have it. But Hyukatake readied the Thirty-fifth Infantry Brigade at Truk to go to Guadalcanal, even as Colonel Ichiki set off on his spectacular mission with the six destroyers commanded by Admiral Raizu Tanaka, which would speed down the Slot and deliver the troops at Taivu Point.

Even though the American operation at Guadalcanal had become an army responsibility, it had begun as a navy show. The airfield was still being built by navy pioneer (construction) battalions, and the navy decided to send some assistance to the marines. On August 15 transport planes dropped food supplies, ammunition, medicines, and word that help was coming. On August 16, the destroyer *Oite* landed supplies and two hundred men of the Fifth Sasebo Special Navy Landing Force, the equivalent of American marines. Other destroyers and submarines cruised the waters of the Slot leading to Guadalcanal. Although the Japanese fired upon them with shore guns, it seemed that they regarded the American presence as so slight as not to be worth worrying about.

Meanwhile, the marines were suddenly afflicted with an epidemic of bacillary dysentery. It affected hundreds of men and quickly made them too weak to be effective. By mid-August one man in five was sick.

On August 17, the marines were bombed by twin-engine bombers carrying delayed-action bombs, which made work on the airfield difficult and dangerous. That day and the next, destroyers shelled Tulagi and Henderson Field. The same day the marines again attacked across the Matanikau and got into a firefight. It culminated in the first Japanese banzai charge, in which sixty-five Japanese were killed. The marines suffered fifteen casualties, eleven of them wounded men. It was a marine victory, and yielded diaries and intelligence material, but also the knowledge that to cross the Matanikau meant trouble.

Then came the night of August 18.

CHAPTER THREE

Makin Diversion

A supporting reason for the Japanese miscalculation about the American strength on Guadalcanal was a raid conducted by the Second Marine Raider Battalion. It took place on the island of Butaritari, or Makin atoll, in the Gilberts Islands on August 17, as the Ichiki detachment was at sea, nearing its Guadalcanal objective. The juxtaposition of events in war can sometimes be misleading. And this was certainly the case at Guadalcanal in the matter of the hit-and-run raid on Makin Island.

After the Battle of Midway, Admiral Chester W. Nimitz, commander of the U.S. Pacific Fleet, began to think in terms of an American offensive in the Pacific. The American war plan—Plan Orange—presupposed a Japanese enemy, just as the Japanese war plan presupposed an American enemy. The navy planners had expected to lose the Philippines, which indeed they had, and to begin the long drive back across the Pacific to Japan through the Central Pacific. In that sense, Admiral King's decision to attack Guadalcanal in the South Pacific was an aberration, although, as it turned out, a necessary one.

When Admiral Raymond Spruance returned victorious from Midway he was swiftly made chief of staff of the Pacific Fleet, and set to work planning the first step on the road to Tokyo. This would be the occupation of the Gilbert Islands, according to the war plan.

The primary problem in the planning was intelligence. The Japanese had captured the British Gilberts Islands colony in the early days of the war. What had they done with it? That was the key question, involving shore defenses, troops, and airfields. American submarines had moved around the Gilberts since then taking photographs, but they were not very informative, and given the Japanese mop-up of so much of the Pacific, air reconnaissance was difficult and not very useful. What was needed was firsthand information, and the training of the marine raider battalions made them ideal for the job of staging a hit-and-run raid to gather the necessary intelligence.*

Lieutenant Colonel Evans Carlson, commander of the Second Raider Battalion, was called in when his troops returned from Midway, where they had been sent to shore up the land defenses. The raider battalion began training on Oahu, where a model of Makin, the largest and most important atoll, was built on the southwest corner of the Hawaiian Island. In July, the Joint Chiefs of Staff approved the plan to attack the Gilberts. Consequently, the training and the planning were speeded up at Pearl Harbor.

Then, as these matters were under consideration, Admiral King stepped in with the demand for the August attack on Guadalcanal. This provided a new reason for the raid on the Gilberts: a diversionary move to throw the Japanese off balance.

Two submarines, the USS *Argonaut* and the USS *Nautilus*, were assigned to the operation, and they trained with the raider battalion. They were big fleet boats, but still they could only carry about a hundred extra men each, and minimal equipment, so Lieutenant Colonel Carlson could employ only about half of his raider battalion. On August 8, the day after the First Marine Division and the First Raider Battalion landed in the Solomons, Lieutenant Colonel Carlson and his men sailed from Pearl Harbor for Makin.

The *Nautilus* arrived first off Makin at three A.M. on

---

*For information about the marine Raiders see Volume 2 of this series, *Stirrings: The American Fight Back*.

August 16. The *Argonaut* arrived later, but both submarines remained submerged that day. They surfaced at 9:15 that night and headed toward shore. It was a blustery night, with rough water and many rainsqualls. But at 2:30 on the morning of August 17, Lieutenant Colonel Carlson and his men inflated their rubber boats, put them over the side, attached the outboard motors, and headed for Butaritari Island in the Makin atoll. The outboard motors fared badly in the stormy saltwater. Soon they began to fail and the men had to paddle.

The raiders were divided into two groups, Lieutenant Plumley's Company A and Captain Coyte's Company B. They were to land on separate beaches. Each would complete its assigned mission (it was hoped), and then return to the beaches that night and go back to the submarines. But the weather conditions changed the plan. Lieutenant Colonel Carlson decided to land all the marines on the same beach, and they moved out while the two submarines sought the safety of deep water four miles off the island, submerged, and waited.

One boatload of marines did not get the word about the change of plans, so went its lonely way to the original beach, but seventeen boats moved to the beach designated by Lieutenant Colonel Carlson and landed safely. At five A.M. the marines were ashore, camouflaging their boats with netting and getting ready to go into action.

On the beach all was quiet. The Japanese garrison consisted of only fifty soldiers, and they were on the lagoon side of the island, while the marines had come in from the open sea. The element of surprise ended at six o'clock in the morning, when one raider accidentally fired his weapon. Carlson assumed that the Japanese had heard and hastened his men on their missions.

Lieutenant Plumley and the men of Company A went across the island to the lagoon side and blocked the road there. They ran into a band of friendly Gilbert islanders who told them that the Japanese were concentrated down by On Chong's Wharf, which was the port area of the island. So the Americans headed that way, but were soon stopped by fire from Japanese machine-guns. The Japanese then attacked, and the Americans killed a dozen of them.

The Japanese had known for some time that the Americans were there, and two ships in the harbor had set to sea. The submarine *Nautilus* shot at them with its deck gun, and left the cargo vessel in a sinking condition and a patrol craft dead in the water.

Lieutenant Plumley's men captured Government Wharf and Government House, where they found some papers, which they preserved. By noon the word that the Americans had landed had spread far and wide; soon Tokyo was informed and Truk and Rabaul. A pair of reconnaissance planes appeared, which caused the two submarines to submerge and stay down. The Japanese radioed back to Jaluit and Mille atoll bases about 250 miles away, and preparations were made for an attack to preserve the Japanese on Makin. At about 1:30 in the afternoon a dozen planes appeared and bombed and strafed the American positions. Two big Kawanishi flying boats delivered reinforcing troops. Carlson learned that the Japanese were also planning to send in more reinforcements.

The raiders not having accomplished very much, were now under attack, and soon a new flight of planes came to renew the air attack. That evening the marines were called back to the beach, and Carlson pondered the problem of how to get them off before they were overwhelmed by Japanese reinforcements. On the beach Carlson counted noses. Eleven men had been killed in the fighting with the Japanese, and twenty had been wounded. That night came the problem of debarkation. The outboard motors were already corroded, jammed up, and useless, so they were pitched into the sea, and the men paddled for the submarines. Seven boatloads made it to the two submarines. But that represented only seventy-three of the two hundred marines.

Many boats capsized, and Carlson organized his defenses ashore. The Japanese launched another air attack and strafed the boats in the water, sinking one and killing the five men in it as they struggled in the water.

Midmorning of the second day found the raiders still in occupation of the island. About seventy men were still there; the rest had made it to the submarines. They held out all day, and finally all but a dozen men were picked up; the remaining men had to be abandoned.

What had the raid accomplished?

Not much. Carlson had gathered some intelligence, but not important intelligence. His troops had shown the American presence, had destroyed most of the port installations, and burned the gasoline supply which could be replenished of course. They had sunk two small craft, and downed two Japanese airplanes, but that was all confetti in terms of the war.

When the submarines returned to Pearl Harbor, the raiders were greeted with a brass band. The veil of secrecy was lifted. Admiral Nimitz thought the navy and the American people needed some good news, so the tale of the marines' exploits was embroidered by the reporters and became heroics. Medals were bestowed.

The Makin Raid had one major negative effect: the Japanese proceeded to fortify the Gilberts, making them a very tough nut to crack in the future. But the raid also had a positive effect: The Japanese could not understand what had motivated the raid that produced so little results. They came to the conclusion that it was of a piece with the attack on Guadalcanal, and they diverted a task force of ships from Guadalcanal to Makin. When the task force arrived it found only the dozen abandoned marines. The dozen fought hard, but nine of them were captured and executed by Samurai sword.

It all remained a mystery to the Japanese. And so, instead of reinforcing Guadalcanal in August with a division or two, which might have changed the course of the war, the Japanese fooled themselves into believing that there were only two or three thousand Americans on Guadalcanal and in the Florida Island complex, and failed to send adequate reinforcements.

In this sense the Makin raid was an enormous success, and contributed greatly to the American ultimate victory on Guadalcanal. For, as will be seen, the Japanese navy performed brilliantly in the island campaign, but its efforts were put to nought by the failure of the army.

CHAPTER FOUR

A Question of Misinformation

The Army will cooperate with the Navy and quickly attack and destroy the enemy in the Solomons while the enemy is endeavoring to complete the occupation. . . . The Ichiki detachment will quickly capture and maintain the airfield at Guadalcanal.

> *Colonel Ichiki's orders from the Headquarters of the Seventeenth Japanese Imperial Army, Rabaul, August 13, 1942.*

Rear Admiral Raizo Tanaka, commander of the Japanese Reinforcement Force of the Eight Fleet, was a very unhappy man. He had protested the orders demanding that he land the Ichiki detachment on the eastern side of the American forces on Guadalcanal. There had been no time to coordinate the activity, no rehearsal for what was in fact an amphibious landing on a hostile shore, and he had presentiments of doom. But it was all to no avail because Imperial General Headquarters had ordered the Ichiki detachment landed, and Admiral Tanaka had no recourse but to follow orders.

The basic problem from the moment the American ships hove into sight at Tulagi and Guadalcanal was the total lack of cooperation between the Japanese navy and army. It had always been thus, since the days of the Meiji Restoration, when the two armed services were established quite separately of each other. The establishment of Imperial General Headquarters just before the war had been a recognition of this deficiency but no real remedy. Each service still reported separately to the emperor, who was commander in chief. On the surface the Imperial General Headquarters functioned in the manner of the American Joint Chiefs of Staff, but in fact IGHQ was dominated by the generals. And the generals and the admirals told each other practically nothing about their separate operations.

On the day the Americans landed, the radio station at the Tulagi seaplane base broadcast until it was knocked out by American naval gunfire, and the naval command at Rabaul knew that the invasion was large-scale. Later in the day they had further proof, from Kawanishi flying boat reconnaissance planes and from pilots of the Twenty-fifth Air Flotilla attack force sent from Rabaul to attack the American ships. The pilots returned to tell of the armada they had seen and the activity on the beaches. But the navy officials at Rabaul and Truk did not pass this information on to the army, because there was no system of liaison and the army did not ask questions.

After the First Marine Division landed on Guadalcanal across the sound, the Japanese fled into the jungle, taking portable radio sets with them. They were in contact with Rabaul and with Truk. In fact they maintained a lookout post atop a ridge overlooking the airfield and reported daily on the American activity there, and on the total American movement around the island. From the information they sent the navy at Truk, Colonel Ichiki had a good idea of the American positions, and when he arrived at Guadalcanal, the survivors had maps ready for him. That was certainly cooperation between army and navy, but at battalion level, not at command level. The problem was that, although Colonel Ichiki was getting an inkling of what he faced, General Hyukatake had none, and IGHQ, which was calling the shots, knew nothing about Guadalcanal at all. At Truk, Colonel Ichiki and the naval authorities had debated the matter of the number of men to employ, but the problem was IGHQ's demand for immediate action, and its lack of knowledge of South Pacific logistics.

And to compound matters still further, Colonel Ichiki and his men suffered from that malaise so common to the Japanese military in 1942, the victory disease. Japanese propaganda had begun to supplement the Bushido belief system, which maintained that the Japanese army was invincible. Colonel Ichiki was a believer, and he was quite ready to go in with a battalion-sized unit, confident in his ability to destroy the Americans.

In the very early minutes of August 19, Colonel Ichiki and a thousand of his men landed at Taivu Point, about twenty-two miles east of the Americans. They were a rush outfit on a rush job, and they had only two mountain guns, about half the heavy mortars they needed, an insufficient supply of ammunition, only one radio, and no field telephones. It was obvious that the planners of Imperial General Headquarters were not taking the American threat seriously, for they had supplied food enough for only a few days.

When day dawned, the marines set out to find out what they could about the landing. A patrol of Guadalcanal Island police set out to the east, and ambushed a party of thirty-four Japanese, including four officers. Thirty-one of the Japanese were killed, and the patrol recovered documents that identified the Ichiki detachment. So General Vandegrift knew that the Japanese army had entered the scene, although he did not know the strength of the landing force. Vandegrift then ordered a strengthening of the defense line on the bank of the Tenaru River. The marines were short of barbed wire, and they were using Japanese rice bags for sand bags, but they built up their positions.

On the night of August 20, the Ichiki detachment attacked to cross the Tenaru. The attack came just after 2:30 in the morning along the east bank of the river. The Japanese opened up with mortars, machine guns, and artillery and followed with a banzai infantry attack. But the troops of the second Battalion of the First Marines held, pouring rifle fire, machine-gun fire, and shells from 37-mm guns into the enemy.

The Japanese withdrew, but attacked again about two hours later, sending a company out through the surf to outflank the marines. They were literally slaughtered by American fire. But still the Japanese machine guns chattered and the Japanese rifles popped. The marines then staged a counterattack. They moved across the Tenaru above the Japanese, made a 90-degree turn, and outflanked them, trapping them in a coconut grove.

Just hours earlier a squadron of marine dive-bombers and other squadrons of marine fighter planes had landed on Henderson Field. At daylight they prepared to operate, and so did tanks on the ground. So the Japanese were surrounded by infantry, hit by tanks, and blasted from the air. Hundreds of Japanese died in this battle, and when it ended, as dusk fell on the Tenaru River, the few survivors returned to Taivu Point to communicate the news of the disaster to Rabaul. Colonel Ichiki, it was said, survived the assault, but could not bear the disgrace of defeat, so committed ritual suicide. The other survivors melted into the jungle to join the survivors of the original marine assault on Guadalcanal and carry out the last part of the orders from the Seventeenth Army: "If [instant victory] is not possible, this detachment will occupy a part of Guadalcanal and await the arrival of troops to its rear. . . ."

This segment of the orders issued to Colonel Ichiki shows very well the difference between the Japanese army's senior officers and the young breed, colonels and below, who had come up within the past few years. General Hyukatake was very much a student of the art of the possible; his orders were conservative and gave a field commander plenty of leeway. But in reading the orders, Colonel Ichiki (and many others at the regimental level) was overwhelmed by his own sense of superiority and his deep belief in the system of Bushido that had been reinvented by the army in its surge to power in the 1930s. Because of General Sadao Araki and other members of the military claque who had invented this fake samurai tradition, Colonel Ichiki really believed that a Japanese soldier was the equivalent of three or four soldiers of other nations. Now, with the failure of the Ichiki detachment's forward element to win a quick victory, Rabaul had learned the sad truth, that they had underestimated the capability and strength of the American enemy.

General Hyukatake, commander of the Seventeenth

Army, then ordered Major General Kiyotake Kawaguchi to bring the Thirty-fifth Infantry Brigade down from Truk to clear the Americans out of Guadalcanal. The Japanese army had still not grasped the idea that this American invasion was anything more than a nuisance action.

To understand this, one must remember that, as an organization, the Japanese army had a tradition of invincibility and no humility. For the thousand years before 1851 Japan had been a hermit kingdom. The Japanese knew of the existence of China, Korea, and India, but of not much else. In modern times the Japanese army had been victorious in all its military operations against China, Korea, Russia, and Germany—or almost all. There were some serous defeats levied on the Japanese in China, and the Communist guerrilla armies, in particular had learned effective methods of causing Japanese defeat. But these losses had been covered up. So had the great defeat by Marshal Zhukov and the Soviet armies in Siberia in the late 1930s, when the Japanese Kwantung Army, unwisely trying to twist the tail of the Russian bear, had lost 25,000 men and untold equipment.

At the regimental level, the young officers truly believed in their own invincibility. It was the most important factor in the Japanese military ambience. But there was, in addition, a physical problem for the Japanese army in the South Pacific. They had an inadequate number of troop transports in the South Pacific to move their troops from Truk and Rabaul to Guadalcanal.

Even as the survivors of Colonel Ichiki's detachment were retreating into the jungle, the second echelon of his force was coming in from Truk, hardly better equipped than the first. They were being brought in one transport, the *Kinryo Maru,* and four converted destroyers, along with the Fifth Special Naval Landing Force, the Japanese equivalent of the American marines.

At the same time Admiral Yamamoto dispatched the battleships of Admiral Nobutake Kondo's Second Fleet and the carriers under Admiral Nagumo to find and engage the American carriers, which were known to have fled south of Guadalcanal.

On August 22, the Americans learned from Southwest

Pacific Command that the Japanese reinforcing force from Truk had been sighted. The marine planes were dispatched to intercept, but they ran into bad weather and could not find the Japanese.

Admiral Tanaka, sighting a PBY scout bomber, reported to Rabaul and was told to turn north and delay his landing. He did, and the Americans missed the reinforcing force that day. Meanwhile, the Japanese battleships and carriers were moving south toward Fletcher's American carrier force.

Fletcher was up to his usual tricks, avoiding action, by sending the *Wasp* carrier group south to refuel. On August 24, Admiral Kondo detached the light carrier *Ryujo* and the cruiser *Tone* and sent them out as bait for the Americans, while the two big fleet carriers, *Shokaku* and *Zuikaku*, prepared to hit the Americans. On the night of August 23, the destroyer *Kagero* bombarded Guadalcanal.

On August 24, all the Japanese elements were in motion: Admiral Tanaka was steaming with his reinforcements toward Guadalcanal, the bait force was steaming south to be seen, and the main Japanese force was steaming on yet another course, to hit the Americans when they found out where they were.

That morning the Americans found the *Shokaku* and attacked, damaging her slightly. A force from the *Saratoga* was much more successful against the *Ryujo*, hitting her repeatedly with bombs and torpedoes so that she sank that night. But that afternoon a scout plane from the cruiser *Chikuma* discovered the two American carriers that were in battle operation, the *Enterprise* and the *Saratoga*, and attacked.

Admiral Fletcher, totally defense-oriented these days after the loss of *Yorktown* and *Lexington*, had put up an enormous combat air patrol—fifty-three planes over the two task forces. The trouble was that the force was *too* enormous; the fighter directors could not handle the radio traffic, radio discipline was bad, and in the confusion the Japanese came through. The fighters shot down a number of attackers— Warrant Machinist Donald Runyan shot down four Japanese planes that day—but the Japanese kept coming. One enemy dive-bomber put a bomb into the flight deck of the *Enterprise*, and then another put one in almost the same place.

The attack did not sink the *Enterprise*—within an hour she was recovering planes—but it did some serious damage by jamming the rudder. The Japanese sent a second air strike against the carriers, but, luckily for the Americans, they did not find them.

When steering control was regained on the *Enterprise*, Admiral Fletcher withdrew, even though he had not suffered much loss of aircraft and he had three operable carriers to the enemy's two, plus many more planes. That night the Japanese searched for the Americans, seeking a night surface engagement, but they did not find them.

On August 24, the Tanaka relief force continued toward Guadalcanal, bringing the rest of the Ichiki detachment and other troops. The American planes now stationed at Henderson Field attacked in the morning. They bombed the cruiser *Jintsu* and the transport *Kinryu Maru*, sank the destroyer *Mutsuki*, and damaged the destroyer *Uzuki*. Admiral Tanaka was ordered to retire to the Shortlands Islands and await developments. There the relief troops were soon loaded into destroyer transports to continue the voyage to Guadalcanal. That day, the carrier *Wasp* came up to seek battle, but her search planes could not find the enemy.

And so the day of August 24 ended, and with it, the battle. The Americans called it the Battle of the Eastern Solomons, and although they were victorious in numbers of ships sunk and damaged, they had not covered themselves with glory by any means. Fletcher's timidity had prevented what might have been a major victory.

At the Shortlands, within a few hours after the battle, the troops destined for Guadalcanal had been reloaded onto Japanese destroyers, which set out again, only to be called back within two hours. The communication problem was at Rabaul, where General Hyukatake ran the Seventeenth Army and Admiral Mikawa ran the naval defense forces. The two men kept issuing contradictory orders. Admiral Tanaka was growing very discouraged, but he obeyed orders and set out with four destroyers and the troops on August 27. Once again he was victimized by Rabaul. As his ships neared the Guadalcanal coast before sundown on August 28, they were promptly attacked by planes from Henderson Field, now augmented by some planes from the carriers which had stopped. Two Japanese destroyers were sunk and one was damaged, and Admiral Tanaka was fit to be tied because of the waste. But Rabaul was looking at the "big picture." Four other destroyers from the Shortlands did manage to land their troops at Guadalcanal that night.

The trouble was—as the navy knew if the army did not— that these destroyer landings only amplified the problem. The reinforcing troops were coming ashore with inadequate supplies—without enough arms or enough food. From the beginning food had been very short for the Japanese and it continued that way.

On August 29 General Kawaguchi and his staff arrived at the Shortlands, eager to get to Guadalcanal and there join the Ichiki contingent and his own forward element of the brigade. He balked at the idea of going in by destroyer: too little space, too little supply capabilty, too little room for field guns. He wanted to go by barge, which was the traditional Japanese army method. They had never had any trouble with it in the past.

But Admiral Tanaka's orders were to send the army in by destroyer, and that was the way it had to be. More troops were embarked in destroyers and General Kawaguchi and his staff remained aboard the *Sado Maru,* which had brought him to the Shortlands. On August 30 another batch of destroyers landed a thousand more men off Taivu. Meanwhile, some of the American transports had returned and landed men and supplies around Lunga.

Every night for a week the Japanese destroyers came down and unloaded men. Meanwhile, both sides were trying desperately to create air superiority. The marines at Henderson Field were joined by planes of the U.S. Army Air Force Seventy-sixth Fighter Squadron, and navy planes from carriers, particularly from the *Enterprise,* which was going home for repairs, leaving its air group behind. The Japanese brought more planes down from the Marshall Islands. During the nighttime hours, the Japanese naval force controlled the waters around Guadalcanal and Japanese planes bombed and strafed the airfield. During the daylight hours, the Allied forces managed to control the airspace; the Japanese came to bomb and lost heavily.

The marines were desperate for fighter planes on Guadalcanal. Actually, there were some fighter planes available after the end of August. The *Saratoga* had been torpedoed and sent back to America, and her aircraft were available. But they were under the command of Frank Jack Fletcher, who did not want them risked at Guadalcanal, but saved instead for his carriers.

At the beginning of September, Major General Kawaguchi was on Guadalcanal, supremely confident that with his brigade he had the strength to recapture the airfield and end the American threat to Japanese supremacy in the area. Providing the backbone of his confidence were his six battalions of troops, more than 6000 men. About a third of these were men of the Ichiki detachment. He had another 2000 men coming in and 1500 additional men from the special naval forces who would operate independently, but cooperatively. So General Kawaguchi decided that he did indeed have the force available to conquer the island. He was dismayed to learn that his last contingent of troops, about a thousand men who were coming by barge, had been caught in the open in daylight on September 5, and thoroughly worked over by American fighters and bombers, losing four hundred troops and most of their equipment.

General Kawaguchi planned his September 13 assault on the airfield for in three parts: a three-battalion attack from the jungle against the airfield, a one-battalion strike across the Tenaru River, and a two-battalion attack from Matanikau across the Lunga River and then down on the airfield from the northwest.

By the first of September, the constant succession of Japanese landings of small forces had brought some confusion to the Americans about the size of Japanese troop strength on the island. General Vandegrift brought the First Marine Raider Battalion over from Tulagi and the First Marine Parachute Battalion too, to strengthen his position. That gave him eight battalions of infantry.

But what was the enemy strength? He did not know. What he did know was that the Japanese kept sending the "Tokyo Express,"—a seagoing train of destroyers—down the Slot almost every night delivering men and supplies. On September 4, Tanaka's destroyers completed their run and then ran into the two American destroyer transports *Little* and *Gregory*, which had taken a large patrol to Savo Island to see what was there. The Japanese sank the American ships. But that day the marines had reinforced the airfield. Admiral John McCain, the commander of land-based air for the South Pacific, warned everyone that air superiority over the island had to be maintained or they might as well give up all hope of holding.

On September 6 Colonel Akinosuka Oka landed on Guadalcanal with the headquarters of the 124th Infantry near Kokumbona, and began to advance toward the Matanikau to get into position for the coming attack on the airfield. At the same time the navy learned and told Imperial General Headquarters that a big American convoy had arrived in the Fiji islands on September 5. The troops aboard must be scheduled for Guadalcanal. This news put the wind up in the IGHQ, and the generals demanded that General Hyukatake attack the airfield at once, before American reinforcements could arrive.

General Hyukatake ordered the attack advanced to September 12. The navy prepared to support the attack with air and sea forces. Far more than the army, the navy had already shown evidence of appreciating the seriousness of the Guadalcanal situation.

On August 8, Admiral Yamamoto had decided the situation was serious enough for him to take personal command in the south, so he had sailed from Japan and begun the campaign of bombing and bombardment that the marines had been witnessing. But early in September, after three weeks of this, Yamamoto had pressed the army to use divisions, not detachments. On September 2, Admiral Tanaka had come to Truk to explain why he was having so much trouble at Guadalcanal. It was the Allied air force on the island, he said, that was continuing to attack his ships.

Yamamoto sent two staff officers to Rabaul to confer with General Hitoshi Imamura, the commander of the regional forces there, and titularly General Hyukatake's commander, and then with the Eleventh Air Fleet, which had been brought from the Marianas to take over the air attack. The

Guadalcanal situation had to be settled on the land, Yamamoto had said. The navy could not dislodge the marines from the island singlehandedly. Henderson Field must be captured. Then the navy could stage an amphibious operation and recapture the island.

On September 7 Yamamoto called a meeting on the flagship *Yamato* of the staffs of the Second, Third, Fourth, and Sixth fleets and the staff of the Eleventh Air Fleet, to make the navy's plans for support of army activities at Guadalcanal on the sea, under the sea, and in the air. The problem was the army's reluctance to pin itself down to dates.

And there was another problem: the Japanese still did not have an accurate idea of the number of marines on the island. General Kawaguchi had 8000 troops, and everyone seemed to think that was a sufficient number. Even Yamamoto agreed to the precept that fighting spirit was more important than numbers. Had not the Japanese so far always accomplished their aims, with fewer troops than the enemy? The American concept of amphibious operations—the need for at least a three-to-one ratio of attackers over defenders—had never occurred to the Japanese.

As the Japanese South Pacific High Command met on September 7 to deal with the Guadalcanal situation, so did Admiral Nimitz fly to San Francisco to meet with Admiral King about this and other matters. Some changes in command were in order: They agreed to move Admiral McCain, who held some of the responsibility for the disaster at Savo Island because his search planes had not located the enemy, back to Washington so that King could assess his fighting qualities. Admiral Aubrey Fitch, who had shown well in the past, would take over the land-based air in the South Pacific.

Vice Admiral Fletcher was on his way out. King did not trust him and insisted that he be relieved of command of the carrier forces and brought back to Washington. It was the kiss of death to Fletcher's fighting career.

The two admirals also talked about Vice Admiral Ghormley. Although they did not know the depth of his negativism, they sensed that something was wrong, and agreed to discuss it soon. From Washington, and even from Pearl Harbor, there was little they could do to control the events of the next few days in the South Pacific. They would have to wait.

On the night of September 7, the First Marine Raider Battalion embarked from the Lunga area on two destroyer transports and two smaller vessels for Tasimboko, where the Japanese were reported to have landed in some strength. General Vandegrift needed information about the enemy to arrange his defenses.

They arrived in the Taivu area just as two American transports, in convoy with a cruiser and four destroyers, came up on their way to Lunga Point to land supplies. The Japanese believed this was a new amphibious landing and ran for the jungle, leaving several fieldpieces behind. So the Raiders landed unopposed, disarmed the fieldpieces and proceeded with their mission. Meanwhile, General Kawaguchi was slogging through dense jungle, literally cutting the way for the three thousand men who were moving to attack Henderson field.

The news of the "new American landing" quickly reached Rabaul where it caused great worry and talk of more reinforcement. Special naval landing forces were put aboard destroyers bound for Guadalcanal, and General Hyukatake considered moving troops over from New Guinea to Guadalcanal.

As the raider patrol moved inland, the Japanese tried to stop them, but in a firefight where the marines were supported by P-40s from Henderson Field, the Japanese were overwhelmed and left twenty-seven dead and several artillery pieces and heavy machine guns. The marines then destroyed large dumps of Japanese food supplies, wrecked radios and other equipment, captured papers, and left for Kukum in the American line. When they got back, intelligence officers discovered something of the plan of General Kawaguchi, and the movement of those three battalions of troops toward Henderson Field.

Lieutenant Colonel Merritt Edson, the First Raider commander, suggested that they fortify a ridge that paralleled the Lunga River south of the airfield. On the south, east, and west slopes of the ridge, it ran to the jungle. On the north it was a gentle slope down to the airfield. It could be a prime defense position. Vandegrift began readying himself for the attack he knew was coming.

He pleaded again for more fighter aircraft, and on September 10, Admiral Nimitz overruled admirals Ghormley and Fletcher and ordered all available carrier aircraft to Guadalcanal. The fighters of Fighter Squadron Five came to the island. They were immediately engaged in combat because the Japanese had also been reinforcing their naval air force at Rabaul.

On September 10 about seven hundred men of the First Marine Raider Battalion and the First Parachute Battalion moved up along that ridge south of the airfield under command of Lieutenant Colonel Edson. Twice on the march they were interrupted by air raids. They strung out along the ridge, and the command post was placed in a gully a hundred yards south, near General Vandegrift's division headquarters. There they dug foxholes and strung barbed wire.

Up above, the Japanese on the mountain watched them come and radioed Rabaul. So the next morning, when the daily bombing raid came to Guadalcanal, the bombing was not directed at the airfield itself for a change, but at the marines on the ridge. Some marines were killed and some wounded by the bombs dropped by the twenty-six twin-engine bombers, but the rest grimly dug in deeper. That night, a patrol sent out to the south reported contact with a long enemy column moving from the east to the headwaters of the Lunga River.

So the Japanese were coming. But where and when? Still nobody in the marine camp knew.

On the afternoon of September 10, Admiral Turner flew to Guadalcanal from Espiritu Santo. As he arrived, so did the announcement of an enemy air raid coming in. It was a fitting greeting, for Admiral Turner brought with him bleak news from Admiral Ghormley, Commander in Chief of the South Pacific:

- The Japanese were amassing enormous naval power at Truk and Rabaul.

- Japanese air reinforcement was coming daily to the airfields around Rabaul.
- Several Japanese transports were lying in Simpson Harbor taking on stores and troops which probably were destined for Guadalcanal.
- Admiral Ghormley anticipated a major air-sea-land effort to retake Guadalcanal within the next ten days.
- Admiral Ghormley could no longer take the responsibility for supporting the marines on Guadalcanal.

In other words, the marines were being abandoned by their commander. They could expect no help.

Admiral Turner stayed overnight and witnessed one of the Japanese naval bombardments, this one directed against the ridge where the marines were dug in. The Japanese seemed to have eyes on the island, and indeed they did— a very active naval contingent in touch with Rabaul every few hours by radio, with watchers stationed on the coast and on the high ground.

Admiral Turner went back to Espiritu Santo, vowing that he would get the Seventh Marine Regiment, which had just been sent to the South Pacific, and deliver it to Guadalcanal. And despite Admiral Ghormley, he did. Within hours the wheels were in motion to bring the Seventh Marines to Guadalcanal.

Admiral Ghormley's report on the massing of Japanese naval and air forces in the South Pacific proved quite correct.

On September 10 Admiral Yamamoto sent his chief of staff, Admiral Matome Ugaki, and several staff officers of the Combined Fleet to Rabaul to be on hand with the army as the operations began. They got there to learn that the operation had been postponed until September 12. This threw the naval calendar out of synchronization, but the army never seemed to understand that, and indeed seemed impervious to comment and warning. On the night of September 11, as the Kawaguchi unit on Guadalcanal was marching to attack, the army officers at Rabaul were holding a party to congratulate one another on the coming victory and recapture of the airfield.

CHAPTER FIVE

Edson's Ridge

In later years it came to be known as Bloody Ridge, possibly because of the work of an alert public relations officer, but the marines at Guadalcanal called it Edson's Ridge, and anyone who served there during those few hours of September 12–14, 1942, might have thought that a whole lifetime passed in that short time.

In the battle of the Tenaru River, most of the marines involved had their first experience with the Japanese as fighters. A few had been on Gavutu and Tulagi in the initial attack, where the Japanese had all fought to the death, but the Tenaru battle was spectacular in this respect. It was a real tribute to General Araki's indoctrination of Japanese school children in the 1930s, and to the harsh Japanese army and navy training that forbade a soldier to give up. The Japanese who tried to cross the Tenaru were slaughtered. Then the marines counterattacked, compressed the Japanese into a pocket in a palm grove, and slaughtered more. In all of about a thousand men, 777 were killed, and fifteen wounded prisoners taken. They must have been so badly wounded that they could not find or use a grenade, because a number of marines were killed when souvenir hunting, or when they tried to take prisoners, by wounded Japanese who shot them or exploded a grenade.

General Vandegrift was amazed at the Japanese performance: "I have never heard or read of this kind of fighting.

41

These people refuse to surrender. The wounded will wait until men come up to examine them . . . and blow themselves and the other fellow to pieces with a hand grenade.''

So the marines who were dug in on Edson's Ridge on September 12 knew what to expect: banzai charges, infiltration, and duels-to-the-death with the Japanese soldiers. It would be that way, they would learn, until nearly the end of the war, when on Okinawa some dispirited Japanese would actually give themselves up. But for almost three years it would be kill-or-be-killed, and the marines who gained from experience took no chances.

Not knowing where the Japanese would strike, General Vandegrift had to make some guesses. The marines under Lieutenant Colonel Pollock held the lower Tenaru River (which the Japanese called the Ilu River). They were joined in the upper reaches by Lieutenant Colonel Mckelvy's Third Battalion of the First Marine Regiment. On the far side of Lunga Point was the western perimeter, defended by Lieutenant Colonel Biebush's battalion. From Biebush there was an open space to the ridge, which was defended by engineers and amphtrac specialists. Then came Edson's Ridge, where the major attack was expected. Behind it was the artillery, General Vandegrift's command post, the engineers, the airfield and, winding down to the Lunga River to the estuary and Lunga Point, a whole series of dumps and installations needed to keep the reinforced division going. If the Japanese could break through at the ridge, they would have a nice grassy plain to go down to the sea.

On September 11, Colonel Jaime Del Valle, commander of the marine artillery, visited the ridge area, and his mapping section began plotting grids and fire zones for the artillery, based on the belief that the ridge would be a focal point of attack.

That day the 105-mm howitzers and automatic weapons were moved to new positions from which they could render the best support to the ridge defenders. At noon that day bombers from Rabaul again came in, and again concentrated their efforts on the ridge rather than on the airfield. The bombing was a warning to the marines that the attack would be aimed at the ridge, and they dug in deeper.

On September 12, General Kawaguchi's troops were

struggling through deep jungle. Kawaguchi had orders to attack that night with naval and air support. By mid-afternoon, Kawaguchi knew it was a mistake to attack so soon. He was still struggling in the jungle. His men would need rest and a chance to regroup below the ridge. But Seventeenth Army Headquarters said "Attack," and so he must. There was no room for argument, no room even for explanation, because in the attack on Tasimboko the marines had destroyed Kawaguchi's communications with Rabaul. The naval forces on the mountain had radios, but Kawaguchi did not have access to them. He and Rabaul were effectively cut off from each other.

Were any further proof needed as to what the Japanese were about, that night, when the "Tokyo Express" came down on its almost nightly run, the cruiser and the three destroyers involved concentrated their naval bombardment on the ridge, not on the airfield.

When the bombardment ended, the Japanese infantry below the ridge began to probe. Kawaguchi did not want to attack, but he knew he must, even though his brigade was very badly confused and the men were not in position. Rifle and machine-gun fire broke out, but were answered from the ridge. Only on the right flank did the Japanese make progress. They cut off one raider platoon, which lost seven men before it could fight its way out and around to the west. They broke through one company, but did not have the resources readily available to exploit the advantage.

The morning of September 13 found the Japanese attacking in small groups all along the line and having the most effect against the paratroops. The fighting proceeded all day. The Japanese made progress, but did not commit themselves to an all-out attack.

At Rabaul, the headquarters of Seventeenth Army was very quiet on the morning of September 13. There was absolutely no word from Guadalcanal. A flight of four observation planes from Rabaul overflew the airfield at Guadalcanal looking for evidence that the Kawaguchi force had captured the field. But they saw a number of American fighter planes on the airstrip and went back to report that the field was still in American hands.

General Hyukatake's staff considered the matter, and de-

cided that General Kawaguchi for some reason must have
delayed his attack for a day. So again, on the night of
September 13, they waited. Since so little was known about
the airfield, the air attacks that might have been made on
the ridge were diverted to the Taivu area, where they had
attacked at Tasimboko a few days before. Twin-engine
bombers flew over the area and dropped their bombs—
squarely on General Kawaguchi's rear echelon, which had
taken repossession of the area after the marine raid.

That night of September 13, the Japanese naval observation plane known to the marines as "Louie the Louse,"
came over and dropped flares, lighting up the island. By
their glow over the airstrip, seven Japanese destroyers bombarded again, but the bombardment was directed to the field,
not the ridge.

Meanwhile, having failed to attain his objective in the
daylight hours, General Kawaguchi was making a series of
night attacks along the marine perimeter. Two reinforced
infantry battalions attacked up the slopes out of the jungle.
The fight lasted until eleven o'clock that night, with the
marine artillery offering the most valuable support. Marine
machine guns, Browning automatic rifles, mortars, and rifles maintained a steady cacaphony as the Japanese launched
one banzai charge after another. Just before midnight, Kawaguchi launched a new assault, but because of the 105-
mm howitzers, it failed. Two hours later came the most
frantic assault of all, with the Japanese coming up the ridge
to within half a mile of the airfield. The marine line was
being badly dented, one company at a time, and reserves
were being committed.

One more assault came against the Second Battalion of
the Fifth Marines that morning, but the artillery broke it up,
and as dawn came, so did the fighters from Henderson Field,
firing machine guns and cannon as they coursed the ridge.
The attack reached a pitch of frenzy, and one officer burst
through into General Vandegrift's command post, waving
his samurai sword which he threw like a javelin to hit one
of the marines. (Another marine killed the officer with a
pistol, ending the immediate threat.) That morning another
Japanese element struck at Lieutenant Colonel Mckelvy's
battalion on the Tenaru River. But with tanks and artillery

and heavy machine guns, the marines threw them back, and they withdrew toward Koli Point.

In the afternoon Colonel Oka brought his smaller independent force against the western marine perimeter, but this attack, too, was repelled. All the way along it was a question of the Japanese having inadequate force and inadequate weapons to accomplish their aims. And it was also a question of planning. Only two-thirds of General Kawaguchi's force was actually engaged with the marines. The others did not get into action because of a basic misunderstanding of the terrain and the logistical problems of Guadalcanal jungle fighting.

On the morning of September 14, General Kawaguchi did not have the strength or ammunition to mount another assault in the face of the planes and 105-mm howitzers. He decided to break through the jungle and began to move south, where there were no trails, his men hacking their way through toward the headquarters of the force at Matanikau. They carried four hundred wounded and left behind nearly seven hundred dead. It took the Japanese troops eight days of struggle through the jungle—eight days during which they ran out of food. Finally they crossed the upper Lunga River, and entered Colonel Oka's area. They reassembled near Point Cruz.

The marines on Edson's Ridge were scarcely in better condition. Their ranks had been riddled in the past two days. Edson's First Raider Battalion, which had landed in the Tulagi area five weeks earlier, was now down from 750 effective men to a little more than 500. The First Parachute Battalion had suffered even more severely. It had come to the Solomons with 377 men and had suffered casualties of 55 percent; just over 150 officers and men were left. The marine reserves, which had been committed to the battle of the ridge, had also suffered severely. The great difference was that the marines had food, while the Japanese of the Kawaguchi unit had none.

Word that the Kawaguchi force had failed to recapture the airfield reached Rabaul on September 15. Admiral Yamamoto, at Truk, was notified, and he warned the army that they would have to bring a sufficient number of troops to the island to do the job. His warning was emphasized within hours, when a number of B-17 bombers landed at Henderson Field.

September 15 was a banner day for the Imperial Navy. That day Commander Takaichi Kanashi, in the submarine *I-19*, found the American carrier force southeast of Guadalcanal and torpedoed the carrier *Wasp*. The same day the *I-15* torpedoed the battleship *North Carolina* and the destroyer *O'Brien*. The *Wasp* sank, while the battleship and the destroyer had to leave the area to undergo repairs. So the Japanese fleet was continuing to score victories over the Allies, even though the army could not seem to pull itself together. When Yamamoto reported that a half a dozen transports were landing men and supplies on September 18, the army answered that it was strengthening its forces. But the only sign of immediate action was the addition of seventeen staff officers to the Seventeenth Army.

Meanwhile, on September 18, the convoy that had reached Lunga Point began unloading the Seventh Marine Regiment. They brought tanks, guns, ammunition, and food—all of which were needed. The act of reinforcement, the landing of the bombers, the coming of more fighter planes, all gave a big boost to the morale of the marines on Guadalcanal, but as could be seen by the war at sea, the shooting was far from over.

CHAPTER SIX

Crisis

The last week of September saw a new effort by the Japanese navy to dominate the sky above Guadalcanal. Admiral Yamamoto ordered a renewed assault, and a hundred fighters and eighty bombers were ferried to Rabaul to step up the effort. But always the Japanese operated at a disadvantage; Guadalcanal is 800 air miles from Rabaul, which meant that the Japanese airmen had to fly four or five hours to reach their objective, then fight, and then try to make their way home. If they were shot down or forced to land, their chances of survival were not very great.

The Americans, Australians, and New Zealanders, on the other hand, were fighting from Henderson Field, and if they were shot down, they had a very good chance of being picked up almost immediately. If they had troubles they could land at Henderson.

So the odds continued to lengthen against the Japanese. On September 28 they sent sixty-two planes to Guadalcanal, and twenty-three of them were lost. The total losses since the August landings amounted to:

Japanese 200 Allies 50

That, however, was not the story the Eleventh Air Fleet gave to Admiral Yamamoto. Of the September 28 raid, they declared jubilantly, "We engaged thirty-six enemy fighters and shot down ten of them. Our losses: nine planes failed to return.''

But that same day, General Vandegrift reported to Admiral Ghormley, ''Our losses: no pilots, no planes, no damage.'' And from a Japanese naval observer on Guadalcanal came a story that supported Vandegrift. The observer had watched thirty-six American planes take off from Henderson Field to meet the incoming Japanese attack, and thirty-six planes land at Henderson when the attack was ended.

There was more bad news from the fleet. The carrier *Taiyo* was torpedoed by an American submarine. The ship as such was not that important—just an escort carrier sent down to Truk to join the fleet in answer to Yamamoto's demands for more carriers after the disaster at Midway— but she had been doing invaluable service in shipping planes from the Central Pacific down to Rabaul.

So that day, September 28, Admiral Yamamoto decided that daylight air raids on Guadalcanal were becoming too expensive in terms of planes and pilots, and moved to halt them. If he needed proof it came from Rabaul, where the Eleventh Air Fleet was asking for replacement planes. While at Truk, Admiral Yamamato realized that these requests and the claims of the pilots did not add up. Something would have to be done to reorganize the Eleventh Air Fleet's efforts.

The opportunity came at the end of September. Vice Admiral Tsukahara, the commander of the Eleventh Air Fleet, came down with malaria and a stomach ailment and had to be sent home to Japan. This helped solve the problem, but again intensified it in an other way. Vice Admiral Ryunosake Kusaka, the new commander of the Eleventh Air Fleet, would need to have some time to learn his job, which would further delay matters.

Also on September 28, Lieutenant Colonel Masanobu Tsuji appeared at Truk. He was a representative of Imperial General Headquarters, and far more important a figure than his lowly rank would indicate. He had just come from Rabaul, where he had laid down the law to General Hyukatake. It was obvious to Yamamoto that Lieutenant Colonel Tsuji had taken charge of army operations on Guadalcanal from a policy point of view. He came with a representative of the Eleventh Air Fleet to indicate what must now be done to secure victory on Guadalcanal.

Lieutenant Colonel Tsuji said that more than a division of troops must be moved swiftly to Guadalcanal, and that they would need five high-speed destroyers—more than were now available—to do it. Admiral Yamamoto was even then complaining about his shortage of destroyers, but when Tsuji told him of the plight of the Japanese troops on Guadalcanal—they were starving—he agreed to do whatever was necessary and to increase the naval bombardment of the island.

That change Yamamoto welcomed as an alternative to the expensive air operations over so long a distance. He would send more cruisers and destroyers to bombard until the army could do its job and capture the airfield.

On the ground, the fighting continued late in September and early October. The Japanese had clustered west of the Matanikau River and were awaiting reinforcements to launch another offensive. With the arrival of the Seventh Marines, General Vandegrift had some extra men, and could contemplate an offensive of his own.

He decided to begin an enveloping movement from the interior, and Lieutenant Colonel Lewis Puller, with the First Battalion of the Seventh Marines, was started on a trek southwest from Henderson Field on September 23. On the shoulders of Mt. Austin, the marines ran into the same terrain that had exhausted the Japanese earlier, and the Japanese assaulted and stopped them. As a result, they had to go north along the Matanikau, instead of crossing. Meanwhile the First Raider Battalion, now commanded by Lieutenant Colonel Samuel B. Griffith, was sent up the Matanikau from the mouth to cross over at Nippon Bridge and join Puller. But the First Raiders were ambushed and failed, falling back to the mouth of the Matanikau on September 27.

Marines from Puller's battalion embarked in Higgins boats and landed west of Point Cruz, expecting to find the First Raiders. They were not there. The Puller troops were then ambushed and surrounded, and got help only when Lieutenant Colonel Puller came up in the destroyer *Monssen* to Point Cruz and covered their withdrawal with a naval barrage. They got out with the help of naval fire and bombing and strafing by planes from Henderson Field. But the offensive could not be counted as anything but a failure; in four days the marines had lost sixty men killed and a hundred more wounded. Still, General Vandegrift wanted to secure the east bank of the Matanikau River, so he assigned six battalions to a new attack.

At the same time, the Japanese were planning a major assault on land at Guadalcanal. General Hyukatake planned to put in 25,000 men, who, he believed could overwhelm the 7500 Americans he thought to be on the island. Once again the Japanese had erred in their intelligence estimates. There were about 20,000 marines on the island by this time.

General Matsurigoto Maruyama, with the Second Division, was ordered to Guadalcanal. One of his first acts was to confer with General Kawaguchi about the failure of his troops and those of Colonel Ichiki to dislodge the Americans from Guadalcanal. Maruyama was so impressed with Kawaguchi's account that he dispatched him on October 6 to Rabaul to report to General Hyukatake and General Imamura, the area commander, that all on Guadalcanal was not as it seemed to be.

On Rabaul, General Kawaguchi briefed the two commanders and their staff, but without any success at all. He told them of the high fighting spirit of the Americans, and of their superior equipment. (The .50 caliber machine gun and the 105-mm mortar were particularly impressive to the Japanese, and so was the Garand semiautomatic rifle, with which some troops were equipped, although the Garand as standard equipment was not issued until several months later.)

But General Kawaguchi found the generals concerned with something entirely different. Just then the Imperial General Headquarters was inquiring of its field commanders—both army and navy—as to their attitudes about the new *bushido*, the code that demanded that every soldier and sailor fight to the death, that admirals and captains go down with their ships, and that army commanders commit suicide if they failed. When they asked Admiral Yamamoto his views, he unloaded them; his view was that the *bushido* approach was the height of stupidity, depriving the services of their most exerienced commanders, and that privately he told his captains to refrain from following the code. That sort of idea did not sit well with the generals, who had been so inculcated with their propaganda that common sense had flown. The generals and staff officers ignored what Kawaguchi was saying, and General Hyukatake prepared to go personally to Guadalcanal to lead the troops. General Kawaguchi returned with him. Thousands of Maruyama's troops were delivered to the island, where they got ready to secure both banks of the Matanikau River and site their artillery there.

But the Americans moved first. On October 7, two battalions of the Fifth Marines attacked along the river, and marched upstream to Nippon Bridge. The Second Battalion of the Seventh Marines, marching inland, reached Matanikau village but found no Japanese. Puller's First Battalion, however, found several groups in ravines, and called for artillery strikes on them. The artillery soon began shelling and the Japanese scrambled up the slopes of the ravines to be met by a a scorching hail of small-arms fire from the marines. Almost seven hundred of General Nakaguma's men were killed in this operation. When General Hyukatake arrived at Guadalcanal he was greeted with the news that the Americans had "decimated" the Fourth Infantry Regiment, and that the Kawaguchi and Ichiki detachments were disorganized and fragmented.

General Hyukatake was beginning to learn. He sent a message to the Thirty-eighth Division, ordering up a regiment, and a message to Imperial General Headquarters announcing that the situation on Guadalcanal was grave.

On October 11 reinforcements for the Japanese on Guadalcanal were moving. So were troops of the 164th Infantry of the Americal Army Division convoyed by an American naval force under Rear Admiral Norman Scott. That night, at what became known as the Battle of Cape Esperance, Admiral Scott led his forces to victory. The Japanese lost the cruiser *Furutaka* and the destroyers *Fubuki*, *Natsugumo*, and *Murakumo*; the cruiser *Aoba* was badly damaged. The force commander, Rear Admiral Arimoto Goto, was mortally wounded. The Americans lost the destroyer *Duncan* in the battle. The American cruiser *Boise* was badly damaged. The cruiser *Salt Lake* and the destroyer *Fahrenholt* were also damaged.

So the battle was an American victory, but while Admiral Goto was fighting, Admiral Joshima landed men, stores, and 150-mm guns near Kokumbona. And since that was the main reason Admiral Yamamoto had sent the forces down to Guadalcanal, he was satisfied with the results.

On October 13, the Americans brought in transports, landed the 164th Infantry, and took out the First Marine Raiders. On the night of October 14, Admiral Yamamoto lived up to his promises to General Hyukatake; the battleships *Kongo* and *Haruna* shelled Henderson Field, set off fuel dumps, wrecked motor pools, and destroyed buildings and ammunition with 14-inch shells. On the airfield they wrecked forty-eight planes, more than half the Cactus Air Force at that moment. The next day planes from Rabaul plastered the airfield again, wrecking the runway. All that was left was a short grass fighter strip, very little gasoline, and little ammunition. Admiral Yamamoto had done his job, and he waited for the army to do theirs.

On October 14, the last contingent of General Hyukatake's troop reinforcement was moving toward Guadalcanal in six transports. They were accompanied by cruisers and destroyers, which shelled the airfield again that night as the transports began to unload their troops at Tassafaronga.

Somehow, with gasoline flown in from Espiritu Santo, the Allies managed to put every possible plane in the air, and some B-17s came from Espiritu Santo to help. They bombed the transports, forcing three of them to beach, and cost the Japanese many men and supplies. But again that night of October 15, the cruisers *Myoko* and *Maya* poured 1500 eight-inch shells onto Henderson Field and facilities.

Admiral Nimitz summed up the Americans' worries that day: "It now appears that we are unable to control the sea in the Guadalcanal area. Thus our supply of the positions will only be done at great expense to us. The situation is not hopeless but it is certainly critical."

Admiral Nimitz knew whereof he spoke, because he had just come down to the South Pacific to see for himself what was going wrong and why. On the way down he had had his first glimpse of the state of affairs at Palmyra Island, where he met Admiral McCain, on his way to Washington. McCain told him about the need for planes and gasoline, and the importance of keeping the Japanese from reinforcing the island.

Next Nimitz met with Admiral Ghormley and representatives of the various branches of the services involved. In the ensuing discussions Ghormley continually indicated his negativism and his view that the whole Guadalcanal operation was a mistake. It was apparent that he agreed with General MacArthur and that he had no realistic appraisal of the situation regarding the Japanese. He told Nimitz that the enemy must have 75,000 men on the island, when in fact they had fewer than 20,000 men at that point.

Had Ghormley been to Guadalcanal? Nimitz asked.

No, said Ghormley.

Then he had better get up there and take a look so he would know what he was talking about, said Nimitz, a little grimly. And he headed for Guadalcanal himself.

But it was nearly at the end of the meetings that Admiral Ghormley made his most serious mistake. General MacArthur had sent a proposal to the Joint Chiefs of Staff for the future conduct of the war against Japan in the south, with himself in command. Admiral King had asked Admiral Ghormley for a plan, and Ghormley had failed to produce one. "I feel that our present operations have not yet reached a point where such a plan and schedule would be worthwhile," he said.

Admiral Nimitz's air officer, Captain Ralph Ofstie, had produced such a plan, and Nimitz left the meetings telling Ghormley to study it and give him his reactions. Nimitz departed with the comment the the Japanese still had the momentum, the morale, and the bases from which to operate offensively.

To Nimitz's eye, the situation was nearly desperate, largely because of American failures in leadership. He did not know that at Truk, Admiral Yamamoto was feeling the same way.

CHAPTER SEVEN

Henderson

At the end of the first week of October both Japanese and Americans recognized the desperate nature of the struggle for Guadalcanal. *The New York Times* noted that it was probably the most important battle that would be fought in the Pacific war.

At Truk, Admiral Yamamoto called a meeting of all his commanders and for two hours the admirals of the Eighth Fleet, the Eleventh Air Fleet, the Combined Fleet, and their staff officers hashed over the plans and ideas for a coming assault on Guadalcanal. Yamamoto said he was prepared to use all the resources of the Combined Fleet in the effort, for "it cannot be unsuccessful." This attitude impressed those at the meeting, but the next day, when Yamamoto conferred with a visiting delegation of IGHQ, representatives from Tokyo, he again had the sense of unreality he always got from these people. They were going to Rabaul, and casually mentioned that they intended to go down to Guadalcanal on October 25, "after the island is recaptured," for an inspection trip.

The army, unfortunately, continued to operate in an intelligence vacuum. One of the Rabaul staff officers actually asked Admiral Ugaki, Yamamoto's chief of staff, "What is a marine?" and did not seem much impressed when Ugaki told him that the U.S. Marines corresponded to the Special

Naval Landing Forces, highly trained and highly motivated Japanese shock troops.

At the top operational level, General Hyukatake seemed to understand the problem. He was talking about bringing five divisions (as many as 75,000 men) to Guadalcanal. But two factors militated against such action. One was manpower; the Japanese were stretched thin, with the China war still gobbling up men and supplies, and every extension of Japanese might was demanding more troops. The other was Japanese army arrogance, which had been stoked by the easy series of Japanese victories to this point. At Imperial General Headquarters, Tojo's commanders did not really believe the South Pacific required any such number of men.

The arrival of the 164th U.S. Army Infantry on October 13 brought the American forces in the Solomons to 27,500 men—23,000 on Guadalcanal and 4500 on Tulagi. The Americans outnumbered the Japanese on the land, but the Japanese still had command of the sea. Every night in mid-October they sent a bombardment force that plastered the island, and particularly Henderson Field, with high-caliber explosive shells, blowing up fuel, ammunition, and food supply dumps and creating havoc on the island.

But the real American problem in the South Pacific was leadership. Admiral Ghormley was on record as doubting the sanity of the whole Guadalcanal operation. That attitude colored his actions; he refused to move troops from New Zealand and French Polynesia to Guadalcanal because he was afraid the Japanese would attack these places. At least once he had told General Vandegrift that the marines would get no more support from him. On October 17 in Washington when a newspaper reporter asked Navy Secretary Frank Knox if he thought the Americans could hold Guadalcanal against the enormous Japanese naval assault, the secretary gave a noncommittal answer. Nobody was certain.

Admiral Turner was doing his best to keep the effort on Guadalcanal going, using desperate means. The major problem in October was obtaining enough aviation gas to keep the airplanes flying. This was solved by unorthodox means; a C-47 air transport could bring in enough gas in one trip to keep twelve fighters aloft for one hour. They came in. The submarine *Amberjack* was made into an underwater supply ship, carrying 9000 gallons of gasoline and ten tons of bombs on each trip. A convoy of cargo ships and work ships was put together, towing barges that each carried 2000 drums of gasoline and five hundred 250-pound bombs. The Japanese planes from the Japanese carriers and Rabaul sank some of the barges and sank and damaged destroyers and other vessels.

When Admiral Nimitz visited the South Pacific, Ghormley's defeatism showed through, and when Nimitz got back to Pearl Harbor on October 15 he had a message from Ghormley, who declared that without enormous reinforcement Guadalcanal could not be held. It was true, but these were not words of confidence and they reinforced Nimitz's suspicions of defeatism. He decided that he had to make a change. At that moment Vice Admiral William F. Halsey had emerged from the hospital (suffering from shingles), demanding a task force and the opportunity to get back into action. Halsey was on a trip to the South Pacific, preparing to take over a task force when Nimitz made his decision on October 15. The next day Admiral King confirmed it. On October 18, Halsey landed at Noumea and was greeted with this message from Nimitz: "You will take command of the South Pacific Area and South Pacific Forces immediately."

"Jesus Christ and suffering Jackson," said Halsey. "This is the hottest potato they ever handed me."

Halsey was the darling of the fleet, and the announcement was greeted with cheers and a general rise in morale.

But a new commander was not the only thing needed, and after his trip, Nimitz saw what was wanted. He persuaded Admiral King to dispatch the battleship *Indiana* with a task group to join the *Washington*, the only American battleship in the area since the *Pennsylvania* had been torpedoed. He ordered the Twenty-fifth Army Division at Oahu to prepare to move to the South Pacific. He sent twenty-four B-17s bombers to Noumea. He sent fifty army fighters from the Central Pacific bases. Twenty-four fleet submarines were ordered to augment the old Asiatic Fleet submarines, mostly little S-boats. The carrier *Enterprise*, having been repaired on the west coast of the U.S. after the Battle of the Eastern Solomons, was ordered to the South Pacific to join the *Hornet*.

* * *

On Guadalcanal, the Japanese were preparing for a new offensive to capture Henderson Field. They had brought in fieldpieces, ranging from 15-cm howitzers to 20-mm anti-tank guns. They had brought in what they (though not Hyukatake) believed to be enough troops to capture their objectives. Pressed by Tokyo and General Imamura at Rabaul, Hyukatake set October 21 as X-Day, the day the assault on Henderson Field would be launched, along with other assaults along the Matanikau River to confuse the enemy.

Lieutenant General Masao Maruyama would command the assault on Henderson Field with 7000 troops. He intended to capture General Vandegrift's command post and the food and fuel and ammunition dumps around the airfield. The right wing was to be led in assault by major General Yumimo Nasu, and the left wing by General Kawaguchi. The Sixteenth Infantry Regiment would be held in reserve.

Then, down on the Matanikau River, where the Japanese artillery was located, the command for the infantry operations was given to artillery commander Major General Teichi Sumoyoshi. One element would attack at the mouth of the river along the marine line, and the other would head upstream and outflank the Matanikau defenders. The Eleventh Air Fleet would provide continuous fighter cover and bomber action, and the navy would provide bombardment and fleet action if elements of the American fleet showed up.

The Japanese army forces began to move toward Henderson Field on October 16. They took with them fieldpieces and heavy equipment, but as they marched, it became obvious that these were a great problem. They bogged down in mud, they slithered off the sides of the track, and piece by piece, the heavy guns and heavy equipment were abandoned. On October 21 they had not reached their jumping-off place and General Maruyama postponed the attack for forty-eight hours, thus throwing off the navy's plans for support.

Admiral Yamamoto had discovered that the Americans had carriers in the area again and he determined to find them and engage them. He had five carriers until the *Hiyo* developed engine trouble, and then had four to the American two.

The army delays caused many problems. On October 21 Yamamoto advised Rabaul that he could maintain the nightly bombardments only until October 23. After that he would need all his strength to oppose the enemy fleet.

On October 23, the army postponed action again, but General Sumiyoshi on the Matanikau did not get the word and kicked off his operation. The Japanese were overwhelmed by American artillery, but at least they called attention to the Matanikau River and away from the Henderson Field area where General Maruyama's force was assembling. This fooled the Americans, but it did not help General Maruyama. His troops attacked on October 24 in a blinding rainstorm that deprived them of unit communications. They were decimated by the American artillery and mortars. Two thousand Japanese were killed. Only 86 Americans died and 119 were wounded in the fighting.

So the Japanese assault had failed, and would have to be repeated.

CHAPTER EIGHT

Attack and Attack

In the deadly struggle for Henderson Field on the night of October 24, the Japanese at Rabaul and Truk had one moment of exhilaration in what was otherwise a negative and frustrating situation for the Japanese army forces. The fact that the defeat and frustration were the fault of the Japanese army itself never seemed to be recognized at Rabaul and in Tokyo, but that was very definitely the case.

The main problem was two-fold: the Japanese did not understand their enemy or his strengths, and they did not understand the geography and climate of these South Pacific islands and the demands they made on strangers.

As noted in the previous chapter, the Japanese had marched across the islands of Guadalcanal to reach the starting point of their attack on Henderson Field. They arrived on October 23, launched the attack—and lost the battle. Exactly how that happened and why has never really been told, but much of the truth lies buried in the Japanese military archives, where, because enough officers survived the soul-breaking Guadalcanal campaign to tell the tale, a Japanese record of the battle exists. Here, from the Japanese official history of the campaign, is the story of what happened to General Hyukatake's assault on Henderson field.

For several days the twenty-ninth Infantry Regiment had been marching through deep jungle, cutting a trail, and piece by piece, abandoning their heavy equipment to try to meet the demands of time. As noted, the attack had been delayed again and again, but not from any perversity or carelessness. General Hyukatake's staff simply had not understood how difficult was the terain of Guadalcanal, up one ravine and down the next, slipping in mud and beset by vines and brush and insects. Some of the men were already sick with fever. They had started out with three days' iron rations, mostly rice and pickled plums, and by October 23 most of the men were half-sick and exhausted from hunger. They did not straggle up to the starting line for their attack until the late morning of October 24, and then they had little time to rest. The attack was scheduled to start at five P.M., but in mid-afternoon a violent rainstorm began. The storm persisted and the attack was delayed and delayed until . . .

At around 10:30 the battle formation began to move out from the jungle toward the grassy plain [where the Americans were located, at the top of the little ridge in defensive positions]. Well below the American positions the scouts encountered barbed wire entanglements which stopped them. All afternoon the ridge had been silent, all afternoon the troops had been assembling in the jungle, sure that they had managed to come up without being detected. But now suddenly one of the scouts heard the first shot, and soon they were under sporadic small-arms fire. The lance corporal leading the scouts on the left reported that at least fifty Americans with several machine guns were behind the barbed wire. How many Americans were up there altogether nobody knew.

Then machine guns began to fire at them. The fire was not continuous and did not seem to be aimed, rather it was area fire, sweeping the grass that covered the flat land from the jungle's edge, and making it most difficult for a planned advance. The fire in front of the Japanese advance was hitting around a hundred meters down the slope from the American position, the leader of the scouts reported. The Twenty-ninth Infantry's First Battalion was in the lead on the left, the point held by the First Platoon with the company commander, closely followed by the Second and Third Platoons. They began worming their way up toward the barbed wire entanglements, and someone saw them, for the machine-gun fire intensified and reached now to the edge of the jungle. The fire was so heavy that some of the men of the platoons drew back into the shelter of the jungle.

The lance corporal who led a squad of five men on the initial patrol reported to the battalion commander and the assistant commander, sketching out the American position four machine guns behind the barbed wire, and now firing at anything that moved, and almost regularly in sweep.

The officer commanding the engineers' platoon came up to confer and the battalion officers looked to him for advice about getting through the barbed wire. Unfortunately, he had to admit, the engineers had abandoned their explosive charges with which they had planned to assault any pillboxes or fortified positions. The march through the steamy jungle had just been too much, too fast. So there was no way of blowing up the barbed wire entanglements. They would have to be approached and the men would have to go over or cut their way through. Since most of the infantry field weapons had also been abandoned on the long trek from the shore, there was no help from that quarter either.

Frontal assault, that was going to have to be the answer.

As these leaders conferred with Colonel Furumiya, a new element could be heard: the American marines' artillery began to fire. They soon saw that it was zeroed in on the grassy plain between jungle and the barbed wire. They watched the high-explosive and marker shells begin to fall, "like a trail of fire on the grassy plain."

The battalion adjutant came up with the plan that would be followed to meet the circumstances. The First Platoon of the First Company would detour to the right to outflank the machine gun on the edge of the American position. As they moved, the army engineers' platoon would work up to the barbed wire and destroy the entanglements, so that the Second and Third platoons could rush forward abreast in the center of the American line and overwhelm the defenses, taking the three other machine-gun positions. The engineers began worming their way forward, stopping and going immobile to avoid the sweep of the American machine guns.

At 10:45 the new attack began. In the darkness vision extended only about ten meters [thirty feet]. The American machine guns still kept up heavy fire, and the only cover was the grass that grew about a foot high, just enough to shield the outline of a human body.

Suddenly the American machine-gun fire and the shelling stopped, and the grassy plain was quiet in the rainy night.

Why had the firing stopped? It was most disquieting, and the tensions of the attackers began to build.

The scouts wormed their way forward to the edge of the barbed wire entanglements to reconnoiter the machine guns. They surged forward in little runs and then dropped prone into the grass. Still there was not a sound from the enemy.

Now the fatigue and hunger and tension began to take their toll of the troops. Some men began to see the enemy all around them, when there was no enemy except at the top of the ridge. The Japanese troops were wet and cold and so hungry they could chew the long sharp grass.

Then, something triggered the whole battalion. Colonel Furumiya heard someone cry:

"Wa!" [Oh!]

And then, almost as a unit, starting from the rear, the men stood up, and began raising their war cry and moving.

"Banzai!" they shouted. "Now, marine, you die," and they began, again from the rear, to push their fellows forward in a wild charge.

The colonel was furious.

"Baka! Fusage!" [Fools! Shut up!] he shouted.

But the men were beyond reason, hysterical, half-crazed with hunger and fatigue, and those behind pushed those before, until a milling mass of soldiers—no longer platoons or squads—charged into the teeth of the American barbed wire before the engineers had finished their cutting job.

With the sounds of the war cry, the American machine-guns opened up again, directed at the noise, not by sight, and as the Japanese soldiers rushed forward they were mowed down like grass. From behind, the Second and Third battalion soldiers took up the cry, not understanding their colonel's demand that they shut up, and the noise gave the Americans more points of aim in the darkness, and the machine guns barked steadily.

The leading platoons rushed forward, to be mowed down, and to to be blown up by land mines on the edge of the barbed wire and by the shell fire coming in from the marine artillery [that was] preset to fire the length and breadth of the grassy plain and into the edge of the forest. The first unit in the frontal attack, the Second Platoon of the First Company, was blown away like chaff. The next platoon came through the bodies to be decimated as well.

As the Japanese closed, the Americans unleashed a new weapon, unknown to the Japanese troops—the deadly flamethrowers, which caught a man and in a second or two turned him into a flaming torch. Coming from left and right, these flamethrowers threw the Japanese soldiers into a frenzy of fear and hatred. As their colonel observed, they came—staggering, many of them, from fatigue and hunger—and they fell before the American positions. Suddenly the advance stopped, completely overwhelmed by enemy machine-gun fire and by the flamethrowers.

The commander of the First Company and four of his men somehow managed to penetrate the American position and get through alive, clambering, rolling over the barbed wire and avoiding the machine-gun fire from the middle guns, but the battalion advance was completely thwarted. Almost the entire First Company was destroyed on the right-hand side of the battle.

On the left, at 11:15 P.M., No. 9 Company and No. 11 Company made their thrust against the machine guns and the left flank of the American position, but again, the Japanese troops broke into a war cry, in defiance of their officers' commands.

"Banzai! Banzai!"

And the American machine guns responded and mowed them down. On the left the bodies piled up at the edge of the barbed wire entanglements. Five men got through, climbing over the bodies of their fellows, but that was all. And others who managed to reach the American position were killed by marines from their foxholes and sometimes in them.

The four enemy machine guns barked ceaselessly. And then, at 11:15, the American artillery bombardment began again, zeroed in on exactly the path of the main element of the regiment. The carnage was dreadful. More men were blown away like chaff and fell along the track. The survivors took refuge off the track in the sides of the jungle, and units were completely disorganized by the bombardment. The men were disoriented and many of them moved back into the jungle away from the fighting.

Colonel Furumiya rallied his officers and passed the word to reorganize for a new assault. The No. 1 track was abandoned as unsafe, because the American artillery had it zeroed in.

The colonel was becoming worried because dawn was near, and he had not attained his objective, the capture of the four machine guns and the forward line, and the rush through the line to Henderson Field on the other side of the ridge.

As the first light of dawn began to sift through the sky, Colonel Furumiya ordered a new attack. No. 10 Company had just reached the line and was standing in the jungle beside the track. The colonel ordered up the Third Battalion. He called the Third Battalion commander and the commander of No. 3 Company. The company would make a passage for the battalion and then bring back the wounded while the battalion broke the enemy line and charged to the airfield. No. 11 Company would follow directly behind No. 10 Company to clean up. No. 3 Machine-gun Company was also ordered to join this attack and support it. The company was brought up under cover of fire, to begin the assault.

The Third Battalion would assault the right side of the line, concentrating on the two machine-guns there and an artillery position beyond.

So the assault began again, but this time the American

line on the right held firmly, and the assault of the Third Battalion, too, was blunted against the barbed wire and under the machine guns. The enemy artillery barrage particularly became terrifying—2400 rounds flying through the air. Bodies were flying everywhere. The leading companies of the Third Battalion were decimated, and more than two hundred men fell in a few seconds as they charged the American positions. No. 10 Company broke completely and fell back to the forest edge.

Colonel Furumiya then called his battalion commanders together and repeated the order: they must assault the line and they must fight through to the airfield. No. 2 Battalion was given this order again in no uncertain terms.

Colonel Furumiya himself decided to lead the charge. He wrapped the regimental battle flag around his body beneath his tunic, and grasped his war sword. He personally would lead No. 7 Company of the Third Battalion into battle. The battalion leader saw an opening. The demolition platoon of the engineers had forced a break near the right-hand machine guns, on the left side of the engineer platoon position. If they moved fast, they could squeeze through before the enemy was able to close up. But now came the enemy artillery barrage again, which delayed the renewed assault another thirty minutes.

It was now about four A.M. and the light was growing fast. Colonel Furumiya, commander of the Twenty-ninth Infantry Regiment, staged an attack on Lieutenant Colonel Puller's position to kick off the attack. Furumiya led his own Third battalion, which in turn led the general Japanese attack. He fired a flare as a signal, and his troops began to move. Followed by officers and men, Furumiya hit the marine line and broke through. Perhaps fifty men made it inside the American lines and pressed forward. But the marines rallied and closed up the gap, and the rest of the battalion was stopped cold. The marines plugged up the holes with elements of the Third Battalion of the U.S. 164th Infantry Regiment. They fought side by side with the marines and stopped every subsequent attempt by the Japanese to break through.

So, as night ended, Colonel Furumiya and his men were driving toward Henderson Field and waiting for the rest of the regiment. They reached the field, and the colonel, who had carried the regimental colors folded up inside his tunic, flew the colors above the field, and sent a runner back through the lines with the news. At field headquarters, General Hyukatake was waiting for just such word, and immediately radioed Rabaul that the long siege was over and had ended in victory.

"Airfield captured."

At Rabaul and Truk the electrifying news was received with great satisfaction. It seemed to justify all the meandering, all the miscalculations, all the failures of the Japanese army here in the past few weeks. Admiral Yamamoto breathed a sigh of relief. Now he could go on to victory at sea, and would not have to expend his ships' energies in the nightly attacks on the airfield.

But that was the only moment of victory, for on the ground in front of the American lines lay the rest of the Twenty-ninth Infantry's First Battalion and they would never attack anything again. The First Battalion of the Twenty-ninth was decimated, and so was the Second Battalion; the marines claimed that they and the army men had killed two thousand Japanese that night. Of course much of the slaughter had been the responsibility of Colonel Del Valle's artillery. As morning came, that artillery moved, recognizing that the attack from the south was the main Japanese effort. New troops were brought in, most of them army soldiers, and the artillery moved some of its guns to bear better on the slopes below the American position.

Although Colonel Furumiya and a few of his men slipped through the marine line, the Second Battalion, which was to follow in close support, was completely frustrated in the attack because it moved too slowly to get through the breach in the American line before it was closed.

The dim light of dawn was turning to day and in the new light the Americans could see the figures of the Japanese moving, so the volume of small-arm, machine-gun and artillery fire increased. "It was as if the torrent became a hail of bullets," said one of the soldiers.

The Second Battalion leader, the Sixth Company, the Second Machine-gun Company and the Fifth Company led a new charge up the rise to the center of the American position, but all in vain. They were swept time and again by hails of fire, and driven back down into the edge of the jungle. The casualties were very heavy.

At 5:30 that morning the rest of the battalion waited for the word from Colonel Furumiya about the airfield, but no word came. The issue was still in doubt now, said General Hayukatake. [Behind the American lines, Colonel Furumiya and a handful of men were still roaming, but now they were trapped inside the American line, and one by one they were destroyed.]

When the attack had definitely failed and Colonel Furumiya did not reappear, representatives from the Seventeenth Army took over and received the report of the Second Battalion leader and his aides. It was a gloomy enough report, but the preparations were made for another attack that coming night, even though the detachments were now scattered in the jungle, where they had fled back from the dreadful carnage of the grassy meadow.

The Twenty-ninth Infantry Regiment was used up, and its commander lost somewhere behind the American lines. It was definitely known that the airfield was still in American hands—particularly when American planes came over the Japanese positions to strafe and bomb. General Maruyama, commander of the Second Japanese Division and entrusted with capture of the airfield, now called in the 124th and 230th regiments. Further back, where there had never been any real doubt about the airfield, the Japanese artillery resumed the fire of its six-inch howitzers on the field.

All day long the two sides planned and moved their forces. The Japanese were planning a two-section assault on right and left with the two regiments. The Americans moved their artillery to new locations and strengthened the line on the ridge.

After dark the Japanese again began to move. The left side of the line, the 124th Infantry, the late Colonel Ichiki's regiment, moved first, but into withering mortar, machine-gun, and artillery fire that decimated that regiment as it moved up to the attack position. The battle was again lost before it began. The 230th Regiment moved to support the 124th, but also took casualties. When the commander reported the sad state of affairs to General Maruyama by telephone and the general learned that Major General Yumio Nasu, commander of the division's infantry, had fallen in a charge, the general ordered the plans for the night attack cancelled. It was Sunday morning. At dawn General Sumiyoshi's six-inch howitzers began firing again on the American positions around Henderson Field. On the field itself, Colonel Furumiya remained, but already he could see that his victory was pyrrhic. His force dwindled constantly; the problem, now that he had not been followed by his men, was either to get back out to fight again, or to destroy an American command post. He failed in both missions. The Second "Sendai" Japanese division, began a retreat. General Maruyama had no reserves left, no food supply, and his men were reduced to scrabbling in the jungle for roots and water and insects. Many men were left on the sides of the track during the retreat, to die of hunger and exhaustion as the survivors retreated through the jungle south of Mt. Austin along the upper Lunga River.

CHAPTER NINE

The Battle of
the Santa Cruz Islands

Admiral Yamamoto had simply been waiting for the Japanese army to carry out its part of the responsibility before clearing the South Pacific of Allied naval power. As Admiral King had recognized from the beginning, the airfield at Guadalcanal was the key to all Allied operations in the area. Once in control of the airfield, the Japanese could control the sea, and then the marines and army troops on the island would be marooned.

Yamamoto was prepared to employ the full resources of the Combined Fleet to achieve this signal victory. That meant five major carriers and one light carrier, five battleships, fourteen cruisers, and forty-four destroyers—against Admiral Halsey's two carriers, two battleships, nine cruisers, and twenty-four destroyers.

Anticipating the capture of the airfield, the Japanese were moving south in the vicinity of Guadalcanal, when they were spotted by an American PBY bomber on October 23, about seven hundred miles north of Espiritu Santo. PBY bombers attacked, but did not score any hits on the Japanese force.

Admiral Halsey knew the Japanese would make a major naval move coincident with the attempt to capture the airfield, so he sent his two carrier groups, built around the

Enterprise and the *Hornet*, to make rendezvous 275 miles northeast of Espiritu Santo. They were to sweep north of the Santa Cruz islands and then move southwest to intercept the Japanese, who should be approaching Guadalcanal. All this was in progress as the Japanese launched the land attacks designed to capture the airfield.

Yamamoto had been fretting about the army's inability to capture the island and had been reassured by the dispatch of General Hyukatake to supervise the job. Just before 1:30 on the morning of October 25 came the welcome news from Colonel Furumiya, transmitted by General Hyukatake's headquarters to Rabaul, and by Yamamoto's liaison officer at headquarters to the flagship *Yamato* in Truk harbor: "Occupied airfield at 11 P.M."

That announcement was immediately transmitted to Admiral Nobutake Kondo's Advance Force. The force included the cruisers *Atago* and *Takao*, under Kondo's direct command, and the carrier *Junyo* of Carrier Division 2 (which at the moment consisted only of the carrier *Junyo*, because the *Hiyo* had developed engine trouble two days earlier and been sent back to Truk for repair). What ships remained of the Japanese Striking Force, the carriers *Shokaku* and *Zuikaku* and the light carrer *Zuiho*, were operating under Admiral Chuichi Nagumo. Nagumo's reputation had been so far diminished, in Yamamoto's eyes, by his many failures that Nagumo was no longer in charge of the carrier operations, but was subject to the orders of Admiral Kondo.

Admiral Yamamoto prepared then for a major naval action, but the preparations were suddenly stopped by the electrifying report that the airfield was still in American hands after all, although fighting continued. However, the navy was soon reassured; General Hyukatake announced that the battle would continue on October 25. The navy at Rabaul would send three destroyers to land reinforcements east of the Americans to assist in the Second Division's attack on the airfield.

On October 25 the Americans had an advantage at sea. Their scout bombers had sighted two of the Japanese carriers at noon, northwest of the Santa Cruz islands and about 360 miles from the Americans. It was too far to launch an attack unless the Americans steamed toward the Japanese to cut the return distance to the carriers. And this is what Rear Admiral Thomas Kinkaid, the senior American officer, decided to do.

At 1:30 in the afternoon a dozen of the scout bombers of the *Enterprise* set off on a search. Not quite an hour later the carrier launched a twenty-nine-plane air strike toward the reported position. Unfortunately, the PBY that had spotted the Japanese fleet had not been able to maintain contact because of rainsqualls, and the Japanese, having seen the PBY and realized that their whereabouts would be transmitted to the enemy fleet, changed course. So both the search and the strike failed. In the process, the Americans lost seven airplanes in crash landings that occurred because they got back to their carrier area after dark and very low on fuel.

That night American shore-based aircraft harried and bombed the Japanese fleet. They found the battleship *Kirishima* and the carrier *Zuikaku*, but they did not manage to score any hits.

On the night of October 25, Admiral Yamamoto told his commanders to prepare for a great sea battle. The army had assured him that it would attack that night, and this time would take the airfield without fail. He expected the American fleet to appear around the Solomons. So seaplanes and land-based airplanes were sent out from the South Pacific bases to try to find the American fleet.

At sea, Admiral Nagumo's great timidity once again came into play on the night of October 25–26, when a PBY attacked the carrier *Zuikaku*. Although it missed the ship, the action worried Admiral Nagumo so much that he again controverted orders to seek battle, by reversing his course and moving north of Guadalcanal. There he awaited definite word that the airfield on Guadalcanal had been captured, so he would not have to worry about land-based air attacks.

Admiral Kinkaid had been instructed, in no uncertain terms by Admiral Halsey that he was to attack. So, as Nagumo retired northward that night, Kinkaid was moving northwest at 20 knots toward Guadalcanal, and the carrier *Hornet* had loaded its deck for what might be the first air strike.

Unlike their performance in the early days, the American

land-based search planes were now doing a very competent job keeping track of the Japanese movement. Just after midnight, a PBY reported the Japanese at a position about three-hundred miles to the northwest of the American fleet. But then the system broke down again. Three hours later a PBY reported the Japanese two-hundred miles out, but the report was delayed for two hours at Admiral Fitch's headquarters before it was transmitted to Kinkaid.

At five A.M. on October 26, Admiral Kinkaid ordered a two-hundred-mile air search to the north. Sixteen SBD dive-bombers went off in pairs, each carrying a five-hundred-pound bomb.

By the time the planes were taking off, Admiral Kinkaid had received the later report of the patrol bombers, placing the Japanese much closer than he had thought. This was confirmed shortly after by a pilot who spotted a Nakajima torpedo bomber (used by the Japanese for search) headed toward the American fleet. The American pilots spotted part of the Japanese fleet—two battleships, several cruisers, and destroyers—and then headed back to their carrier, passing the Nakajima again. It had been on the same mission with the same results, and had found the American fleet for Admiral *Kondo*. At 6:30 Kondo had the report, and the carriers began preparing to launch their planes. As they were doing so, just before seven A.M., a pair of American search planes found the *Zuikaku* and *Shokaku* less than two-hundred miles northwest of the American fleet. As they watched, Zeros came after the two American bombers. The bombers shot down two of the Zeros; the rest then dropped into cloud cover and disappeared. But Lieutenant Stockton B. Strong and Ensign Charles R. Irvine also found the light carrier *Zuiho* and attacked it with their five-hundred-pound bombs. Both bombs hit, starting fires in the *Zuiho*'s after section. Flight operations had to be suspended. The *Zuiho* had already launched planes for the first strike against the Americans; it would not be able to send a second. Though Zeroes went after the Americans, they failed to get them, and the gunners of the American planes claimed to have shot down two Zeros. Other planes on search found and bombed the cruiser *Tone*, but did not score any hits.

The Nakajima torpedo bomber had reported the American

position to the Japanese fleet command correctly. Just after seven o'clock that morning, the first air strike from the Japanese got off the decks of the *Zuikaku* and *Shokaku*, and the two carriers were preparing a second strike.

Although the Americans had drawn first blood in the battle with their attack on the *Zuiho*, they were slow to get their first big air strike off, taking twenty minutes more than the Japanese had done. The strike came off piecemeal: twenty-nine planes from the *Hornet*, then nineteen from the *Enterprise*, and then twenty-five more from the *Hornet*. So the planes were strung out for miles, creating a real disadvantage for the Americans, because the lack of formation made them a good target. A dozen Zeroes pounced on the *Enterprise* group, shooting down three Wildcat fighters and damaging one other. The Zeroes then shot down three American bombers and damaged a fourth, losing three Japanese fighters. So the Americans had already lost eight of their attack planes before they even approached the target, while Japanese had lost just three.

The Japanese air strike was the first to arrive, heading into the two carrier systems. The *Enterprise* was accompanied by the battleship *South Dakota*, the cruiser *Portland*, the special antiaircraft cruiser *San Juan*, and eight destroyers. A few miles southeast, the *Hornet* was encircled by a bristling array of antiaircraft guns aboard the cruisers *Northampton* and *Pensacola*, the antiaircraft cruisers *San Diego* and *Juneau*, and six destroyers. Overhead, covering the whole area, were thirty-eight fighters of the American combat air patrol.

But now the second disadvantage caused by the slowness of the American reaction came into play. The Japanese were coming in, but they were passing American planes going out. The fighter director of the *Enterprise*, who was running the air defense, could not separate one from the other until nearly nine o'clock, when the Japanese were only a few miles out. The combat air patrol saw the Aichi 99 dive-bombers coming in at 17,000 feet. Soon it became apparent that the American combat air patrol was too close to the carriers. Thus the air battle would be fought over them, rather than in front of them, and the chance of the Japanese scoring hits was much greater.

The first element of the combat air patrol went after the Aichi bombers, from 22,000 feet. They shot down several bombers, but by diving they put themselves out of the battle because they lost their altitude advantage. Other American fighters were too far away from the Japanese planes when they started to dive, and those around the *Hornet* were too low to get an altitude advantage.

At nine o'clock, the *Enterprise* managed to find a rain-squall and turned in to it, finding safety for a while. But the *Hornet* was out in the open under clear blue sky. Down came the dive-bombers. The antiaircraft gunners manned their guns, and shot down several bombers. But one of the enemy planes put a bomb into the starboard section of the flight deck, and two near misses buckled plates and started leaks. The Japanese squadron commander, wounded, dove his plane into the carrier. He hit the stack, glanced off, and bounced onto the flight deck, where his bombs exploded.

So the dive-bombers came in high on the *Hornet* and the torpedo bombers came in low, putting two torpedoes into her side. The carrier spouted a column of smoke, and skidded to a stop, her engines paralyzed and all power and communications broken down. Stopped, the *Hornet* was easy prey: three more five-hundred-pound bombs slammed into her deck and a flaming dive-bomber smashed into the bow, blowing up near the forward elevator shaft and doing more damage. In the end, most of the Japanese bombers were shot down. The Japanese later admitted to the loss of twenty-five planes over the *Hornet,* but the carrier had been very seriously damaged.

In just ten minutes the battle was over for the *Hornet,* it seemed. Damage-control parties scurried along the decks trying to save the carrier. The bombs had detonated down as far as the fourth deck and fires were blazing everywhere. The torpedoes had given the carrier a list of eight degrees.

At first the Japanese had identified but a single American carrier, the *Hornet,* and so the *Enterprise* remained untouched. Meanwhile, more than fifty planes from the *Hornet* approached the Japanese carrier group. At 9:15 A.M. the fifteen dive bombers and four fighters of the leading wave sighted the enemy cruisers and destroyers that led the force, but passed over them, even though nine Zeros of the Japanese combat air patrol attacked them. The Wildcat fighters went after the nine Zeros and engaged. Two American fighters were shot down, but the bombers had passed the carrier and went on.

At 9:30 the first strike found the *Shokaku* and the *Zuikaku*. Then the combat air patrol over the carriers struck the American bombers, which had no fighter protection. Two of the dive-bombers were shot down, and two were damaged so badly that they had to run for home, but eleven of them bored in against the Japanese. They put at least three bombs (some say six) into the flight deck of the *Shokaku*, starting fires, destroying the flight decks' ability to operate, and wrecking the hangar on the second deck.

The *Hornet*'s torpedo bombers got lost that morning and did not find the carriers, so they attacked the cruiser *Suzuya*, but did not torpedo any ship. The *Hornet*'s second wave of dive bombers also missed the aircraft carriers. They attacked the cruiser *Chikuma*, damaging her so badly that she had to head for the repair base at Truk.

The planes of the *Enterprise* failed to hit anything. Half their number had been shot down earlier, and those that were left tried to bomb the battleship *Kirishima*, but missed. The American torpedo bombers launched at a heavy cruiser, but also missed and headed back toward the American fleet.

By 9:30 that morning the first phase of the Battle of the Santa Cruz Islands was over, and both sides were expending much of their effort to save their carriers. The *Zuiho* was badly hurt, and so was the *Shokaku*; neither could launch more planes. But on the Japanese side the *Zuikaku* and the *Junyo* were still intact.

On the American side, the *Hornet* was in bad shape, but not yet near sinking, and the damage-control party leaders thought she could be saved. Two destroyers stood by and worked their fire hoses, and by ten A.M. all the fires seemed to be under control. The cruiser *Northampton* was about to take her under tow, and the chief engineering officer told the captain he thought he could raise steam in three boilers and thus get the *Hornet* under her own power later in the day. The *Enterprise* had not been hit at all.

* * *

But the battle was not yet over.

At five minutes past ten, a single Aichi dive-bomber appeared out of nowhere and screamed down to attack the *Hornet*. Her pilot missed, and nearly hit one of the destroyers standing by, then screamed away.

Where did this pilot come from?

He was a part of a group of bomber pilots who were just then attacking the *Enterprise*, twenty miles away, and he either had gotten lost or had decided to have one carrier all for himself.

The result of this attack on the *Hornet* was to make everyone in the *Hornet* task force nervous, and to delay the salvage operations.

The *Enterprise* task force faced its first real unpleasantness when the Japanese submarine *I-21* fired a salvo of torpedoes at her. They missed the carrier, but hit the destroyer *Porter*. She went dead in the water, and her crew was taken off the ship. The torpedo had gone into the fireroom, killing fifteen men of the black gang and wrecking the ship's propulsion system. If she could be saved it would have to be by towing.

The *Enterprise* and the battleship *South Dakota* had the most modern radar and brand-new 40-mm antiaircraft guns, mounted in groups of four, which were capable of putting up a virtual hail of fire. But if the radar was functioning, the radar men were not, and neither were the fighter-control directors, because the second Japanese air strike came in, and while the radar of *South Dakota* was picking up the planes when they were fifty miles out, the combat air patrol made no effort to intercept. The first anybody aboard the carrier knew of the attack was the moment when the dive-bombers started down and the antiaircraft guns opened fire.

If the air department was not on its toes that day, the gunners, particularly of the *South Dakota*, definitely were. They fired rapidly and accurately and ultimately claimed to have shot down thirty-two planes, (they were given credit for twenty-six). The Japanese bombers dropped twenty-six bombs against the *Enterprise*, hit it twice, and had a near miss with another.

The first bomb struck the carrier near the bow at an angle, plunging downward fifty feet, then passing out the side of the ship and blowing a parked aircraft over the side. The second bomb hit behind the forward elevator; it broke in two on the hangar deck and went down, killing many men on other decks. The third bomb was a near miss, but it damaged the engines and started leaks. Then fourteen torpedo planes joined in the attack, but by this time the fighters were in action, and they shot down or harried the Japanese torpedo pilots. Nine planes actually dropped torpedoes. The *Enterprise* managed to turn to miss four or five of them. Three others hit the cruiser *Portland*, but they were all duds. One torpedo-plane pilot, with his "fish" still fixed to his aircraft, made a suicide dive on the destroyer *Smith*, killing twenty-eight men and wounding twenty-three, but not putting the ship out of commission.

Forty minutes went by, and the *Enterprise* was now troubled with friends. The aircraft of both the *Enterprise* and the *Hornet* now had nowhere to go but the deck of the *Enterprise*, and the damage-control crews were still fighting fires and damage there. Also, a periscope was reported just as the pilots were asking for landing instructions, which made life even more complicated.

Moments after eleven A.M. another strike—this one form the carrier *Junyo*—was picked up by radar but unseen in the growing cloud cover. Once again the ship's radar and combat air patrol goofed. At 11:20 the ship reported "no unidentified aircraft." Exactly one minute later the dive-bombers began to drop. The gunners, with their new Bofors guns, took a large toll of the dive-bombers (eight out of twenty), but one bomber put its bomb so close to the carrier that it did more damage. Stragglers then appeared, and bombed the *South Dakota* and the cruiser *San Juan*, doing considerable damage though not stopping the ships.

That, finally, was the end of the attack. Now the *Enterprise* could begin to take aboard planes. It was a slow process, as the forward elevator was inoperative, and because it was slow, a number of planes, out of gas, had to splash nearby, but their airmen were picked up by destroyers. Thirteen dive-bombers were flown to Espiritu Santo to make way for the *Hornet*'s planes.

By 11:30 that morning the carrier *Hornet* was on the end

of a towline, successfully being towed by the cruiser *Northampton* after one false start in which the towline broke. Rear Admiral George D. Murray moved his flag to the cruiser *Pensacola*, and the wounded and the sailors not needed for damage control or towing operations were moved to destroyers. It seemed that the battle was over, and the job now was to get the crippled ship back to Espiritu Santo.

But again, the Japanese took the initiative. Admiral Nagumo was steaming away from the enemy, when the *Shokaku* became hors de combat and he had to transfer his flag to the destroyer *Arashi*. That put Nagumo out of command of the *Zuikaku*, which was probably the best thing that had happened to the Japanese all day. The aggressive Rear Admiral Kakuji Kurita took over, at just about the time that Admiral Kondo ordered the undamaged carriers *Junyo* and *Zuikaku* to turn toward the enemy, go in, and "annihilate" him. The Japanese now suffered from the loss of aircraft, because about a hundred of the enthusiastic fighters had been shot down, but Admiral Kakuta managed to put together a strike from the *Junyo*, made up of five of her own planes and ten that had been inherited from the crippled *Shokaku*. So, as the *Shokaku* and the *Zuiho* steamed north to safety and repair work, the Japanese carried the battle again to the Americans.

Once again, when the Japanese reached the task force, there were no combat air patrol planes to stop the attack. At 3:15, when the Japanese torpedo planes came in, the *Northampton* slipped her tow to be able to maneuver. The anti aircraft cruiser *Juneau* was too far away to be of any help. The *Hornet* lay virtually dead in the water, no aircraft supporting her, her crew mostly off the ship—the perfect target.

So she was torpedoed, and the water began to flood into her after engine room. The starboard list increased to 14 degrees. Soon the Japanese dive-bombers came, but not one of them scored a hit, nor did the antiaircraft gunners bring down any enemy planes. Then another formation of Japanese bombers appeared and put another bomb on the corner of the flight deck. A third wave came at five P.M. and to drop one more bomb on the carrier's flight deck.

That evening Admiral Kinkaid made the decision to sink

the *Hornet*, not because she could not be saved, but because Kinkaid was afraid of another Japanese attack next day, and did not want to risk the last American carrier in the Pacific. In the words of Admiral Halsey on another occasion, Kinkaid had decided to "get the hell of of here," and Halsey concurred. So destroyers fired eight torpedoes against her, but although she absorbed three more torpedo hits (the rest were duds or false runs), she would not sink. The destroyers tried gunfire, pouring more than four hundred rounds of five-inch shells into the carrier, but she still would not sink.

By this time the Japanese were coming again, seeking a night engagement, and the American fleet moved out to escape. The Japanese came up to the blazing carrier and considered trying to salvage her. But she was burning fiercely and the decision was made to sink her. The destroyers *Makigumo* and *Akigumo* put four torpedoes into the *Hornet*, and finally, she sank.

That night Admiral Kondo prepared for another battle, but during the night American bombers attacked the Japanese force, damaging the destroyer *Teruzuki* and nearly torpedoing the *Zuikaku*. The next morning, the Japanese continued to steam ahead to find the Americans until early afternoon, when Admiral Yamamoto called on the Kondo force to retire to Truk. It was apparent that the army's new attempt to seize the airfield on Guadalcanal had failed. Kondo's ships, which had been out for two weeks waiting for the army to succeed, were low on fuel and ammunition, and a great number of aircraft had been lost. Yamamoto called Kondo back to regroup.

The Americans had more trouble. The battleship *South Dakota* collided with the destroyer *Mahan* while trying to avoid a submarine. The battleship *Washington* was attacked by the submarine *I-15* and one torpedo came within four hundred yards of hitting her, but the warhead exploded prematurely. With all this danger, Halsey ordered the force out of the area and it split, in two, half going to Noumea and half to the New Hebrides.

When the battle was over, knowledgeable Americans commented that the Japanese airmen were losing their competence; given the sitting ducks that had been provided time after time, they had achieved relatively few hits, particularly on the *Enterprise*, which was completely surprised by two attacks. And it was true. Others claimed that the big change had come about because of the growing efficiency of American guns and gunners; this was also true, but it was not the real reason, as the kamikaze attacks would prove later on. The problem for the Japanese at this stage of the war was the tremendous loss of trained pilots that had begun at Midway and been continued in the air battles for Guadalcanal and New Guinea. The Japanese pilot-training program was not moving nearly fast enough to provide skilled airmen for an attenuated war. Admiral Yamamoto had recognized this potential problem even before the war started.

What was also apparent was the incompetence of the American fighter-director system to give warning and protection to carriers. They were still operating independently of one another. During Admiral Fletcher's command of the force earlier, he had put so many planes in the air that the fighter director could not tell friend from foe, and this had occurred again at Santa Cruz to an extent. But more important was the way the aircraft were used, bunched up and in the wrong place at the wrong time. Something new had to be added if the carriers were not to end up as ducks on a millpond for the enemy gunners and bombers.

So the Battle of the Santa Cruz islands was a Japanese victory, but Admiral Yamamoto was not impressed by the trumpets. He recognized that Guadalcanal was a vital struggle, and that it must be won if the war was not to be lost. He saw that the army had failed to do its part of the job. Henderson Field remained in American hands as a base for the defense of Guadalcanal and a jumping-off point for the rest of the Solomons. The air flotilla at Rabaul had been replaced by the Eleventh Air Fleet, but the fleet had lost so many planes and pilots that it was now almost entirely manned by replacements, and the quality of the replacement pilots was continually dropping.

The Japanese army now knew that it had failed, and vowed to put the matter to rights. Admiral Yamamoto could see that it was very late in the game, the balance of air power had changed, and now the balance of sea power was threatened by the Allies. The war had been in progress for less than year, and already Yamamoto's prophecy was looming as a possibility for Japan: that first would come easy victories, but then, when American industrial might was turned to war, the situation would be reversed. Examining the growing strength of the Allies in the Guadalcanal area, Yamamoto realized how little time he had left to produce a victory.

CHAPTER TEN

The Balance at Sea

In Tokyo, Emperor Hirohito realized that there was serious trouble in Guadalcanal and that the Imperial Army had so far failed to live up to expectations. It was seen as the most serious army failure to date. The emperor called attention to it by issuing a new Imperial Rescript congratulating the navy but pointing out that Guadalcanal presaged "this critical turning point in the war." The army's failure was its first in history, barring the unfortunate Nomonhon incident against the Russians.*

As November began, both sides set about reinforcing their troops on Guadalcanal. Every week the air strength at Henderson Field was increased; Now B-17s operated from this field as search planes, penetrating into the Northern Solomons, and marine, navy and army air units were all stationed at Henderson. The marines clamored for more air support, but the single airfield at Guadalcanal, plus the rough fighter strip, could scarcely accomodate what the marines wanted. There was a plan to build an additional airstrip elsewhere on the island, but it would have to wait for more favorable conditions. From the American point of view it was still an

*In 1938 the overexuberant young officers of the Kwantung army had decided to slice off a piece of Siberia and attack a Soviet outpost at Nomonhon on the Manchurian border. The Soviets had responded with force, and Marshal Zhukov came to prominence as the victor; before the incident ended, the Japanese had lost more than a division of troops, about 25,000 men in all.

unsatisfactory situation, because the Japanese still had naval superiority in the area even if they no longer had air superiority over Guadalcanal. Still, transports and supply ships coming to Lunga Roads were at risk. General George Geiger, the marine air commander on Guadalcanal, had only twenty-nine combat-ready aircraft, which were being held together with parts from salvage. But soon some of the planes from the *Hornet* and *Enterprise* would come to the island to relieve the shortage. And soon, too, more army planes would arrive.

From the Japanese point of view, the problem of resupplying the Japanese troops on Guadalcanal, now made up all elements of two divisions, plus remnants of several special attack detachments (Ichiki's, Kawaguchi's, and Sasebo Naval Special troops) loomed very high. In the Japanese system, the army usually provided its own transports and supply ships, which were then conducted by the navy to their destinations. But the shortage of supply vessels had already caused the navy to undertake the resupply and reinforcement of the army by transport destroyer.

The highest-ranking naval officer really close to the situation in Guadalcanal was Vice Admiral Gunichi Mikawa, commander of the Eighth Fleet, who was stationed at Rabaul. At this point he recommended that reinforcement of the troops be delayed, pending massive reinforcement of the air forces at Rabaul and the achievement of air superiority over the Solomons once more. That way, the Japanese could bring in their reinforcements and resupply at will, without the losses they had been suffering. But it was obvious that Imperial General Headquarters did not recognize the real problem, because IGHQ ignored the proposal, and instead moved to bring more troops to Guadalcanal as quickly as possible.

Nor did the Navy General Staff in Tokyo recognize the changing balance of naval power that was on its way. After the Battle of the Santa Cruz Islands, Admiral Nagumo had claimed the destruction of all the American capital ships in the Guadalcanal area. Admiral Yamamoto could really do nothing to stop this type of boastful behavior. He complained about it, but in Tokyo the public information office kept giving out overoptimistic reports of every engagement, and the army believed these tales because relations between army and navy were never close enough for the army to have the inside story.

So IGHQ ordered the Twenty-first Independent Mixed Brigade sent to the Seventeenth Army and the Fifty-first Division to proceed to Rabaul for backup. Troops would be sent to the upper Lunga Valley and west of the Matanikau River, and they would launch a new assault on Henderson Field. Colonel Toshinaro Shoji, who had retreated to Koli Point with two thousand men, was ordered to start marching on November 3.

For the next week, marines and Japanese fought ground actions, but what both were waiting for was reinforcement. The 38th Division was on its way to help the Japanese. It would be brought in by destroyer on six nights—sixty-five destroyer loads and two cruiser loads of troops to Western Guadalcanal.

On the American side, the reinforced Eighth Marine Regiment and the Second Marine Raider Battalion were being brought to Guadalcanal to strengthen U.S. forces. Construction of a new fighter strip was also begun west of Kukum.

The Americans staged a drive in the first days of November, but while many Japanese were trapped and killed, the results were anything but conclusive. More important, on November 9, when Admiral Halsey returned to Noumea from a visit to Guadalcanal, he was met with the intelligence that elements of the Japanese Combined Fleet had just sailed from Truk, and that there was new naval activity at Rabaul and in the Shortlands.

At sea in the South Pacific on November 9, 1942, were two American supply convoys. The first, coming from Espiritu Santo, was a group of three cargo ships escorted by Rear Admiral Norman Scott in the cruiser *Atlanta*, accompanied by four destroyers. The second, coming from Noumea, was a group of four transports, escorted by two cruisers and four destroyers, under Rear Admiral Daniel J. Callaghan.

Admiral Scott's group arrived at Lunga Roads on November 11. It was met by planes from the carrier *Hiyo* shortly after its arrival. The attack produced only minor damage to one ship, the destroyer transport *Zeilin,* and cost the Japanese a number of precious planes and pilots. Later in the day twenty-seven twin-engine Japanese bomers bombed Henderson Field again.

The second American reinforcement convoy arrived on November 12. Ironbottom Sound was then filled with American warships—five cruisers, eleven destroyers, and two minesweepers—to protect the transports from submarines and to aid in antiaircraft fire. On November 7 the navy cargo vessel *Majaba* had been torpeded here by the submarine *I-20,* so the concern about attack was no joke.

At six o'clock the morning of November 12, the first submarine alert was sounded six miles from Lunga Point. The destroyers moved into action, though they did not make another contact, and the cargo vessels unloaded as rapidly as possible. At one o'clock in the afternoon, a coast watcher at Buin reported that enemy fighters and bombers were on their way to Guadalcanal. Admiral Turner stopped the unloading and got his ships moving toward Savo Island so they could maneuver at sea and fight off the the air attack. In this, they would have the help of the warships and the Cactus Air Force, which had just been augmented by a new squadron of marine aircraft.

The defense was very successful. The Japanese attacking force was decimated by antiaircraft fire, while not a single torpedo got through to the invaluable transports. The only serious damage was to the cruiser *San Francisco,* which was struck by a damaged plane that steered into the ship, causing fifty casualties and wrecking the fire-control radar system.

That same afternoon the transports moved back to unload more supplies, protected by their five cruisers and eleven destroyers. Meanwhile, the air search planes had been out and were reporting sighting many Japanese ships that seemed to be converging north of Guadalcanal. One report put two battleships, a cruiser, and six destroyers, two hundred miles to the northwest. Another put five destroyers slightly to the west of the first group. A third report said that two carriers and two destroyers had been sighted moving 265 miles to the west.

From these reports Admiral Turner deduced that the Japanese were coming again to bombard Guadalcanal. It was a critical juncture: almost all the supplies and men of the transports had been unloaded, but they were still on the beach and vulnerable. The obvious countermesure was to oppose the enemy with the available cruisers and destroyers, and so Admiral Turner ordered Admiral Callaghan to seek battle, and then ordered the transports to get away from Guadalcanal. Darkness of November 12 found the transports moving out, bound for Espiritu Santo, and Admiral Callaghan putting his ships into battle formation. It was a long line of ships; four destroyers in the front, five cruisers in the middle, and five destroyers in the rear. (The others had gone to escort the transports to Espiritu Santo.) By ten P.M. the American force was moving into Ironbottom Sound.

Admiral Turner's guess about the Japanese intentions was correct. At 3:30 that same afternoon, two Japanese battleships, a light cruiser, and fourteen destroyers had joined up seventy miles north of Indispensable Strait, and begun heading toward Guadalcanal. Their mission was to destroy the planes and facilities at Henderson Field by naval bombardment. They were hampered by bad weather, but expected to arrive off the island and begin the bombardment at 1:30 on the morning of November 13.

Just before that time, a radar operator aboard the American cruiser *Helena* made a contact, identified as ships, about ten miles away from the American vessels. Admiral Callaghan turned the American line of warships toward the enemy, and soon the two forces were rushing at one another at a combined speed of 40 knots. At 1:41 the destroyer *Cushing* sighted Japanese destroyers crossing the line and turned to use torpedo tubes. The rest of the column turned with the *Cushing*, the other skippers believing that the Japanese destroyers were American ships, and that they were just turning to avoid collision. No order was given to fire, and so no one did, and the Japanese ships disappeared, now warned that the American enemy was nearby.

At 1:45 Admiral Callaghan suddenly decided that these *were* enemy ships and give the order to open fire. Just then there was nothing at which to shoot, but five minutes later the Japanese searchlights began to find the American vessels surprisingly close to them. One destroyer focused a light on the bridge of the cruiser *Atlanta*, and this became the aiming point for several Japanese ships. The *Atlanta* was also firing on Japanese ships by this time. A Japanese salvo landed on the bridge of the *Atlanta*, killing Admiral Scott and everyone on the bridge of the cruiser. The torpedoes from the Japanese destroyers then struck the cruiser and she went dead in the water.

The battle was a scene of complete confusion, with Japanese and American vessels crowded together, firing as fast they could, and not even sure of what they were firing at. The *Cushing* was firing on a Japanese destroyer to her starboard, but she was hit repeatedly and slowed down. She fired six torpedeoes at the battleship *Hiei* but none of them hit. Then a Japanese searchlight focussed on the *Cushing*, and Japanese shells pounded into her until she was a wreck.

The American destroyer *Laffey* was just behind the *Cushing*, and she too fired torpedoes at the battleship *Hiei*, but the distance was too short, and the "fish" did not have time to arm, so the warheads did not explode and the torpedoes bounced harmlessly off the *Hiei*'s sides. Then, two 14-inch salvos from the battleship and a torpedo did for the *Laffey* and she began to sink. She was abandoned immediately, but exploded as she went, down, killing many of her survivors.

The destroyer *Sterett* was third in the American column and the destroyer *O'Bannon* was fourth in line. The *Sterett* was firing as she moved, but an enemy salvo hit her steering and disabled it. Then a shell on the foremast knocked out her radar. She still managed to fire four torpedoes at the *Hiei* and the *O'Bannon* fired two more. But again, they did not connect.

The *Hiei* and the battleship *Kirishima* then turned away from the battle; they were too close to the American ships and it was feared that their guns would depress. The *Hiei* had taken more than fifty shells from American gunfire, so she was moving slowly. The destroyer *Akatsuki* had sunk. The destroyer *Yudachi* had suffered an internal explosion and gone dead. Three other Japanese destroyers had been damaged, but were still operable.

The *San Francisco* had been firing (at the *Helena*, unfortunately) and Admiral Callaghan, seeing this, issued a cease-fire order, so the American ships all stopped firing. The Japanese did not. The *San Francisco* was hit, and Admiral Callaghan and his staff were wiped out as the bridge was devastated.

Hit by a torpedo, the cruiser *Portland*'s steering was damaged, and she began to travel in a circle. The *Helena* was firing at several ships and continued to do so as the Japanese turned away. The *Juneau* took a torpedo and went dead in the water. Then at the end of the line were the destroyers *Aaron Ward*, *Barton*, *Monssen*, and *Fletcher*. The *Aaron Ward* had to stop and change course to avoid collision with the *Helena*. She fired and apparently sank one Japanese destroyer, but then was herself hit and damaged; by 2:30 in the morning she, too, was dead in the water.

The destroyer *Barton* launched four torpedoes, but then received two herself in quick succession. She broke in two and sank. The *Monssen* made the mistake of switching on fighting lights, which made the ship a very good target, and she was deluged with nearly forty Japanese shells. She became a burning hulk in a few moments and then exploded. The *Fletcher* fired on several ships, scoring hits. This ship seemed to bear a charmed life; she went through the whole action without receiving a scratch.

Dawn rose on eight crippled ships between Savo Island and Guadalcanal; five of them were American, three, Japanese. The *Hiei* had lost her rudder. The *Portland* was steaming in circles, but managed to sink the damaged *Yudachi*. The *Atlanta* made it to Lunga Point, but later in the day, had to be scuttled as unsalvageable. The Americans, licking their wounds, tried to salvage what they could, but that day, Friday the 13th, was an unlucky one for the cruiser *Juneau*. The submarine *I-26* found her as she was limping south and torpedoed her. The *Juneau* exploded, apparently with no trace of survivors or wreckage. Actually, a hundred men had survived the explosion and were clinging to debris in the water, but no message was sent to Halsey to organize rescue work, and so the men were ignored. Three paddled to a small island, four were found by a PBY, and one man was rescued eleven days later from a raft. That was all.

So the action at sea ended on November 13. It was followed by air action. The damaged *Enterprise* contributed nine torpedo bombers and six fighter planes to the Cactus Air Force that day. The torpedo planes found the crippled *Hiei* and crippled her still more with torpedoes, so that later in the day other Allied aircraft had to attack and sink her northwest of Savo Island.

Who actually won the battle?

On the face of it, the Japanese had won it without question. They had sunk the cruiser *Atlanta*, the cruiser *Juneau*, and five destroyers and had damaged several other American ships at a cost of just one battleship and two destroyers to themselves. But it was a cheerless victory for the Japanese, because Admiral Nobuyaku Abe had failed in his mission to bombard Henderson Field and set it up for the army's coming attack. Admiral Abe was relieved of command. That same day, November 13, Vice Admiral Mikawa left the Shortlands in the cruiser *Chokai*, with four heavy cruisers, two light cruisers, and six destroyers to bombard the field. Rear Admiral Raizo Tanaka was also at sea, charged with an amplified mission of the "Tokyo Express." He was to bring eleven destroyers and eleven transports laden with troops to reinforce the Japanese at Guadalcanal.

The Americans termed the ensuing engagement part of "the Naval Battle of Guadalcanal," but it was really quite a separate engagement from that of November 13, and fought for different reasons.

The Battle of Guadalcanal had been forced on the Americans when they were not ready, but the sacrifices the Americans made there had given Halsey a chance to bring up his major capital ships: the damaged but serviceable carrier *Enterprise*, (her forward elevator still jammed) and the new American battleships *Washington* and *South Dakota*. They were moving rapidly toward Guadalcanal on November 13.

Admiral Yamamoto had ordered Admiral Kondo that day to pick up the remnants of Abe's force, which included the battleship *Kirishima*, the light cruiser *Nagara*, and four destroyers, to support the transports' landings. Out there somewhere, too, and on their way were the Japanese carriers *Junyo* and *Hiyo*. The most important naval action of the campaign was about to be joined, to see if this Japanese attempt to give massive aid to the troops on Guadalcanal could succeed. If so, it seemed quite probable that the Japanese would ultimately capture Henderson Field, and that is what Admiral Yamamoto counted on.

At Noumea Admiral Halsey's attention on November 13 was concentrated on the plight of his damaged ships, but by midday he realized that something else was afoot. He had the report of a massive effort by the Japanese to reinforce Guadalcanal—by far the largest effort yet, and for once the Americans were in a position to act swiftly. The *Enterprise* and the two battleships were within range of Guadalcanal.

On the afternoon of November 13, Admiral Halsey ordered Admiral Kinkaid, the task force commander, to send the battleships ahead to prevent the bombardment of Henderson Field. It was already too late. The battleships were still 350 miles from Savo Island, and could not reach Guadalcanal before the morning of November 14.

And so the Japanese were not completely frustrated in their efforts against Henderson Field, although delayed for a day. All that lay between the Mikawa force of cruisers and destroyers when they hit Savo Island, were the American PT boats. For thirty-seven minutes the Japanese cruiser and destroyer force bombarded Henderson Field. They were no substitute, however, for the battleships that had not yet arrived. They destroyed one bomber and seventeen fighter planes, and they damaged thirty-two planes, but at the end of the bombardment the field was still operational. One American illusion had been rudely shattered, however. At dark on the November 13, the Cactus Air Force had reached its all-time high in strength; more than a hundred operational planes were on the field. But the Japanese had knocked that force back down to size.

At two A.M. on November 14, Admiral Shoji Nishimura, having expended all the amunition available, and led the Japanese ships back to Savo Island to join the Mikawa force, and the ships then retired to the Shortlands Islands base Islands.

So far it seemed to be another Japanese success. This was a great cause for concern in Washington, where there was very little understanding of the salient fact that the Japanese were being worn down by attrition. Their air power at Rabaul was desperately strained. The loss of destroyers was also troubling Yamamoto a great deal. And too many of his carriers were laid up for repairs, a serious drawback when he was facing the long air haul to attack Guadalcanal. He was counting on this reinforcement mission to resolve some of his problems of overextension and get the army into shape.

On the morning of November 14 the American search planes were out early and, at seven A.M., discovered two large groups of ships heading down the Slot, 150 miles northwest of Henderson Field. One of these groups was the retiring Mikawa force. The American bombers damaged the cruiser *Kinugasa* and the light cruiser *Isuzu*. When planes from the *Enterprise* found this group of ships later, they sank the *Kinugasa* and damaged the cruisers *Chokai* and *Maya* and the destroyer *Michishio*. But all these ships and the *Isuzu* made it safely into the haven of the Shortlands.

The importance of the Japanese reinforcement mission and the confidence that Yamamoto had in the Japanese ability to control the sea were indicated by the fact that the "Tokyo Express" was coming with its reinforcements in broad daylight. At seven A.M., planes from Henderson Field sighted Admiral Tanaka's reinforcement group of destroyers and transports heading south. At 8:30 in the morning two scout bombers from the *Enterprise* found the Tanaka force and attacked a transport, scoring one hit and a near miss. One of the bombers was then shot down by Zeros from the carrier *Hiyo*'s combat air patrol.

At Henderson everything that could fly and fight was put on the line that morning, and shortly before noon seven torpedo planes and eighteen dive-bombers, escorted by a dozen fighters, went after the supply convoy. Just before noon they attacked and damaged several of the eleven transports that had started on this vital mission.

An hour later, seventeen dive-bombers with fighter protection attacked the transports again, and then strafed. One transport broke in half and sank. Another hour went by. The transports and their eleven destroyer escorts were still steaming toward the landing beaches in the Japanese territory of Guadalcanal. The attacks became almost continuous. At 1:45 twenty navy and marine dive-bombers found the convoy, and were followed by another ten bombers. Then a flight of fifteen B-17s from Espiritu Santo attacked. Zeros from Rabaul had come down to help the naval force, but the B-17 gunners fought them off and claimed to have downed several fighters. The big bombers also scored another hit on a transport, as well as several damaging near misses. At 3:30 eight bombers from the *Enterprise* and a dozen fighters attacked the convoy sixty miles southwest of Savo Island. By this time, three of the transports were dead in the water or sunk.

Admiral Tanaka forged onward, stopping only to transfer men from the sinking transports to the eleven destroyers. Three more flights were dispatched from Henderson Field that afternoon. One flight of navy bombers attacked without escort, and the Zeros had a field day with them, shooting down three of the seven planes. Two more marine flights also attacked that afternoon, and by nightfall only four of the eleven transports were still moving with their escort of eleven destroyers, many of those destroyers now carrying surviving troops from the wrecked transports that had been left behind. The Japanese Thirty-eight Division, which was being sent to build up General Hyukatake's Guadalcanal force to a point where it could take the airfield, was already a shambles, with much of its equipment lost in the transports that were left behind or sunk.

Admiral Tanaka had his instructions—to deliver those transports to Guadalcanal—and he was determined to do so, although by the night of November 14, he had only four transports left and most of them were damaged. Later, the Americans would wonder why the supply mission was not delayed, the transports turned about and sent back to the Shortlands for reorganization. But the fact was that Admiral Tanaka had firm orders from Admiral Yamamoto: succeed with the supply mission at all costs. So his orders to the command were: beach on Guadalcanal and unload. The transports would be lost, but their invaluable supplies and men would not. So the Japanese transports came in to the beach that night. As morning came, the Americans saw the last of them; the *Yamatsuki Maru*, beaching herself not far from the *Kinugawa Maru*, and the *Hirokawa Maru* and *Yamaura Maru*, which were already unloading.

Dawn brought a succession of American and other Allied air attacks on the hapless transports, attacks that persisted all day long. American shore batteries on Guadalcanal also fired on the ships, and at least one American destroyer spent several hours firing on the transports.

The result of this last day of destruction was the almost total failure of the supply mission, although four transports had gotten through. Only about 2000 survivors of the Thirty-eight Division were landed, and fewer than 300 cases of ammunition and 1500 bags of rice. An ammunition dump, set up during the night, was hit in an American attack and exploded.

The result of this failure was Japan's abandonment of attempts to reach Guadalcanal with transports. It was the most important decision of the attenuated battle, because it meant that there was now no chance the Japanese could win the island.

CHAPTER ELEVEN

The Battleships

The main reason that Admiral Tanaka had persisted—in the face of repeated air attack—in bringing the transports to Guadalcanal was that Admiral Yamamoto had planned that the arrival of the Thirty-eighth Division to reinforce General Hyukatake on Guadalcanal would be accompanied by a major new bombardment of the island from the sea. After Admiral Abe's bombardment mission of November 12 had failed, Vice Admiral Nobutake Kondo was assigned the task of destroying the enemy's capacity to fight from Henderson Field. On the morning of November 14, he set out from the base near Ontong, Java, with the battleship *Kirishima*, the cruisers *Atago* and *Takao*, the light cruisers *Nagara* and *Sendai*, and ten destroyers to do that job. The Japanese were headed for Santa Isabel Island, from which they proposed to enter the Slot and steal down on Guadalcanal. During the afternoon the American submarine *Trout* attacked the flotilla, but its torpedoes missed.

At the same time, on November 14, American Rear Admiral Willis A. Lee was off Guadalcanal with the new American battleships *Washington* and *South Dakota* and four destroyers, seeking a surface action with the Japanese. Admiral Lee's intention was to frustrate the Japanese attempt to bombard Henderson Field.

Just after ten P.M. on November 14, the lookouts of the light cruiser *Sendai* sighted enemy ships north of Savo Island, heading into Ironbottom Sound. Thereupon Admiral Kondo issued an attack order, and went chasing the American fleet.

The two American battleships discovered the *Sendai* on their radar and opened fire. The *Sendai* then put up a smoke screen and ran. Meanwhile, the American destroyers had discovered other elements of the Japanese force. The *Walke* began firing on the Japanese destroyers *Ayanami* and *Uranami*. The Japanese ships seriously damaged the *Walke* and in a few minutes she was falling out of line. The destroyer *Preston* began firing, but was soon hit by enemy shells and disabled. Then the *Walke* and the *Benham* were put out of action by Japanese torpedoes.

The American battleships were having their problems, with crews that were not very well trained. The *Washington* could not seem to get going in this battle, and the *South Dakota* suffered a power failure that knocked out her radar. By 11:30 that night all four American destroyers were out of action, disabled by Japanese gunfire and torpedoes. The *Walke* blew up and sank, the *Preston* was abandoned to fire and sank, and the Benham limped back toward base but ultimately had to be sunk by the *Gwin*, which then headed home to Espiritu Santo.

The two Japanese heavy cruisers and the Japanese battleships found the *South Dakota*. She was illuminated by a destroyer's searchlights, the big ships began to fire on her. But the radar of the *Washington* also found the Japanese battleship *Kirishima*, and hit it with at least nine sixteen-inch shells and about forty five-inch shells. In seven minutes the *Kirishima* was a wreck. The cruisers *Atago* and *Takao* were taking a beating from the battleship's guns. Admiral Lee then chose to disengage, having lost two destroyers, and did not go after the two Japanese cruisers and the two light cruisers. Instead, he headed for Noumea, with the battered *South Dakota* (which had been hit about fifty times) trailing behind.

Admiral Kondo abandoned the mission of bombarding Henderson Filed. He rescued the crew of the *Kirishima*, and then scuttled her northwest of Savo Island in the early hours of November 15. The destroyer *Ayanami*, badly damaged in the fight, was also sunk by the Japanese.

So the battle ended, a victory for the Americans in spite of their losses, because they had again frustrated Admiral Yamamoto's plans to smash Henderson Field.

CHAPTER TWELVE

For the Moment, a Draw . . .

On November 16, 1942, the Imperial General Headquarters staff still believed the Japanese army could win on Guadalcanal. In fact, IGHQ insisted that Japan would win, and so informed Emperor Hirohito. For the Japanese, but not for the Americans, the South Pacific campaign in the Solomon Islands and the Southwest Pacific campaign in New Guinea were one and the same. At sea, Admiral Yamamoto was responsible for both, and in the air, his Eleventh Air Fleet at Rabaul bore most of the responsibility for the campaign to take Port Moresby. The army put the newly created Eighth Area Army under the command of Lieutenant General Hitoshi Imamura. Lieutenant General Hyukatake's Seventeenth Army on Guadalcanal and Lieutenant General Hatazo Adachi's new Eighteenth Army in New Guinea were also placed under Imamura's command.

Admiral Yamamoto pulled some strings in Tokyo and finally got rid of Admiral Nagumo, his air commander, who had been a thorn in his side for so long. The new commander of the carrier force was Vice Admiral Jisaburo Ozawa, a man much more to Yamamoto's liking. Yamamoto also got a promise that the army would begin to supply some of the aircraft for the theater. Until this time the responsibility for the air defense of the whole area had fallen on the navy.

Now the army promised to supply planes and pilots in a new cooperative program. In fact, however, the army did not have the slightest concept of the the theater's aircraft needs and the army pilots were not trained for long flights over the sea, so the offer of cooperation was not very meaningful in a practical sense.

This revised Japanese plan for the South and Southwest Pacific envisaged a holding action on Guadalcanal until January, and then a major two-pronged drive to take Guadalcanal and Port Moresby simultaneously.

As for the Americans, they, too, had some reorganizing to do in November. The First Marine Division was very tired, having been in continuous action since the first week of August. So plans were made to bring in the Sixth Marine Regiment from New Zealand and the 182nd Army Infantry of the Americal Division from New Caledonia. The First Marine Division prepared to leave Guadalcanal.

On November 18, General Vandegrift started a new attack in the hope of wiping out the Japanese Seventeenth Army. Brigadier General Edmund Sebree, the senior army officer, was ordered to drive into the western sector, using the 182nd Infantry, the 164th Infantry, and the Eighth Marines, with the First Marines in reserve. The marine artillery was assigned to support the drive to the Poha River line.

The drive began on schedule but was almost immediately stopped cold in the Point Cruz area. The 182nd Infantry crossed the Matanikau River on a footbridge, then started a long march with full packs. The soldiers were not used to the deadly Guadalcanal climate and many of them collapsed on the march. But finally the 182nd reached its first day's objective. On the second day more troops moved up, but on the third morning the Japanese attacked and hit the two separated American battalions on the flanks. The 164th Infantry was rushed up to close the gap, but could not advance. The Eighth Marines were called in, and got a big surprise. The word had been out that the Japanese were dispirited and beaten. Not these Japanese. They set the Eighth Marines back on their bottoms. On November 23, General Sebree consulted with General Vandegrift, who realized that the plan had been premature, and called off the assault.

At the end of November General Alexander Vandegrift was replaced as land commander on Guadalcanal by Major General Alexander Patch, because the marines were leaving the island and the army, generally speaking, was taking over.

Although the Japanese morale was recovering because of promises from Rabaul of reinforcement and supply, General Hyukatake was in no position to make a major assault. He was confident that he could hold, given supply, until the reinforcements came in at the end of the year. Admiral Turner wanted a new air base on Guadalcanal on the other side of the island, and the Second Marine Raiders were sent to clear a way for the establishment, but soon it proved impractical to build over there, and the plan was abandoned. So a sort of stalemate developed—except that it was a deceptive stalemate. The Americans were building up everywhere—on the sea, in the air, and on land. The Japanese were going nowhere.

The Japanese position was outlined at the end of November. The Second Sendai Division of 10,000 men, had been reduced to 5000 effective troops. The Thirty-eight Division, which had been brought in by Admiral Tanaka in the transports and transport destroyers, had also been reduced to about 5000 men by the attrition resulting from the battle of the transports. Colonel Ichiki's Twenty-eighth Infantry Regiment was cut down to two understrength battalions, and General Kawaguchi's Thirty-fifth Brigade amounted to only about a thousand men. The naval special troops and the engineers who had occupied the island before the Americans came numbered about 1500. Altogether, battle, attrition, and disease had reduced the force of Japanese sent to Guadalcanal from more than 25,000 men to about 15,000 at this time.

Hyukatake was told that the Fifty-first and Sixth divisions, about 20,000 men, would soon be coming to Rabaul for use in the area. So would the Twenty-first Mixed Brigade and a huge contingent of army air force planes, including a whole air division. But these were all promises, not actuality.

One thing was certain. At long last, prodded by the navy, the army had begun to understand the true importance of

Guadalcanal. On November 26, when General Imamura took control of the Eighth Area Army at Rabaul, he made a speech to his troops, which was distributed throughout the command, in which he put the truth on the line: "The outcome of the Greater East Asia War, which will decide the fate of our Empire depends solely on this area army."

But from the outset, Imamura faced a serious problem at Guadalcanal. The failure of the eleven-transport convoy to deliver its full quota of supplies and equipment to the troops on Guadalcanal caused an almost immediate crisis. The force in the island had been augmented by several thousand troops, but only a few loads of supply had come ashore—so little that the men of the Thirty-eighth Division were forced to subsist on the supply of the troops who had been fighting. By the end of November all the rice was gone, all the noodles, all the meat. The men were beginning to forage for food, eating wild animals and wild plants. Malaria was bringing down hundreds of men, and dysentery soon struck. The sick list was greater than the ready list. The situation swiftly became desperate.

Rear Admiral Raizo Tanaka, the destroyer commander, was entrusted with the resupply of Guadalcanal at this point. There were serious restrictions to be faced. Chief among these was the strength of the Allied air forces operating out of Henderson Field, which had brought about the destruction of the eleven-transport convoy. At the end of November that Cactus Air Force was stronger than ever, with 150 planes operating out of Henderson Field. Even if Tanaka had been willing to repeat the experiment of bringing in a transport convoy in the face of Allied air control of the island shores, the Rabaul command now faced a serious shortage of army transport ships. Tanaka would have to do the job using his destroyer transports, which did not have unloading facilities for large amounts of supply, even if they could carry them.

So the admiral devised a system of swift unloading. Metal drums were filled with medical supplies and food, leaving enough air space to assure buoyancy, and then sealed. The drums were stacked on the decks of the destroyers, linked by ropes, and when the destroyers came up the crews would throw the strings of drums overboard, while small power boats came out from the shore to pick up the supply chains. Thus the destroyers would never be stopped in the water, prime targets for the Allied bombers, but would be in fighting trim all the time.

The first destroyer supply mission was set for November 29, and that day Admiral Tanaka led eight destroyers out from the Shortlands base toward Guadalcanal. Six of the eight ships were loaded with supplies, and to save weight all but one torpedo for each tube was removed on these six. The other two destroyers were loaded with normal ammunition and torpedoes.

CHAPTER THIRTEEN

The Battle of Tassafaronga

The Japanese were using three methods to resupply their troops on Guadalcanal. First, Admiral Tanaka was assigned the task of running the aerial blockade with his destroyers. On November 30 and every four days thereafter, he was to deliver supplies to Guadalcanal by destroyer transport.

Second, the Japanese Sixth Fleet, the submarine force, was told to make boats available for supply missions; this became a major factor in their work as of November 1942.

Third, the army worked at its own supply, running food and ammunition and medicine along the chain of the Solomon Islands in barges, which traveled together in groups with soldiers aboard to defend them.

Some transports were still operating in the Solomons, although no more were sent to Guadalcanal. On November 27, Allied airmen discovered two transports moving out of Munda, on the island of New Georgia, obviously having brought supplies to that place, probably for transshipment by barge to Guadalcanal. And indeed, that was a part of the reason they were there; another was the decision of the Imperial High Command to build up the remainder of the Solomons, and in particular to strengthen air bases in the area.

* * *

After the air battle of the eleven transports and the two naval battles around Guadalcanal in mid-November, the American naval force was badly diminished and had to be rebuilt to take care of ship losses. Admiral Halsey established a new cruiser force, which finally came under the command of Rear Admiral Carleton H. Wright in the flagship *Minneapolis*. He had also the cruisers *New Orleans*,. *Northampton*, and *Pensacola*, the light cruiser *Honolulu*, and four destroyers. The force was called Task Force 67.

Through the breach of the Japanese naval codes, Halsey's command learned that a Japanese supply convoy would be arriving at Guadalcanal off Tassafaronga on the night of November 30. Halsey then ordered Task Force 67 to intercept. Admiral Wright set sail from Espiritu Santo just before midnight on November 29, traveling at 28 knots to make the six-hundred-mile journey to Guadalcanal. The cruisers' floatplanes were dispatched ahead to the seaplane base at Tulagi to await the arrival of the cruisers and then be available for scouting the enemy and illuminating the battle zone.

On the night of November 29, Admiral Tanaka and his destroyers left Buin, on the southern end of Bougainville Island, bound for Tassafaronga. The eight destroyers traveled north through Bougainville Strait and east toward Roncador Reef, and then turned south through Indispensable Strait.

The next morning they traveled slowly to keep out of the range of Henderson Field bombers until after darkness fell on the 30th. That afternoon Admiral Tanaka learned that a Japanese reconaissance plane out of Buin had spotted the American task force coming up toward Guadalacanal. The Americans learned that day that eight Japanese destroyers were missing from the anchorage at Buin, but no one know where they were going.

On the afternoon of November 30, Admiral Tanaka had more news: an American supply convoy had reached Lunga Roads, and a half-dozen American destroyers were with the transports. So, as Tanaka approached Guadalcanal that evening, he was prepared for a fight. That evening, as Admiral Wright came up to Lengo Channel (which separates the reefs off Florida Island from Tasimboko and Taivu Point), he met the U.S supply convoy, now unloaded, going the other way. He commandeered two of its destroyers to add to his force. So Task Force 67 moved through Lengo Channel, four destroyers in the van, followed by the five cruisers, and two destroyers bringing up the rear.

At eleven P.M. Admiral Wright's force entered Ironbottom Sound. A few moments later his radar operators had their first indication of the presence of an enemy force nearby. Forty-five minutes later, Admiral Tanaka's supply force was west of Savo Island, moving south toward Tassafaronga, and Admiral Wright's force was just north of Henderson Field.

Having no radar, Admiral Tanaka's destroyers were unaware of the enemy. But the admiral expected trouble and warned, "There is a great possibility of an encounter with the enemy tonight. In such an event, efforts will be made to destroy the enemy without regard for the unloading of supplies." His force entered the waters of Guadalcanal just after 10:45 and slowed to 12 knots, preparing to release the floating drums in their strings, and moving parallel to the shore, two miles out.

Admiral Wright was now expecting the floatplanes of his cruisers, sent ahead to Tulagi, to be in the air scouting for him. They should have been up for a long time. But the floatplanes were still in Tulagi harbor, taxiing along the water but unable to get a lift-off because there was no wind. So Admiral Wright had no "eyes" except his radar.

That radar had indicated the enemy's presence as early as 11:15, and the destroyer squadron commander had asked permission to fire torpedoes. That permission was delayed, but finally given. The American destroyers began firing torpedoes four miles from the nearest Japanese destroyer. The *Fletcher* launched ten torpedoes, the *Perkins*, eight, and the *Drayton*, two. The *Maury*, whose skipper was uncertain and did not have fire-control radar, did not launch any at that point.

So the Americans knew where the enemy was, and by radar had started firing on the still-unsuspecting Japanese. A moment later the cruisers began firing their guns, also by radar; eight-inch shells, six-inch shells, and five-inch shells were hurtling through the air.

In truth, the Americans were having a lot of trouble with

their fire-control radar, and the *Pensacola*'s radar was not the new type, so she faltered. The *Honolulu* was delayed in firing. But soon all the cruisers were firing. The enemy should have been pulverized by torpedoes and gunfire. But even if the enemy was completely surprised, he was far from pulverized. Admiral Tanaka became aware of the Americans when a lookout on the flagship reported two torpedo wakes directly ahead. At the same time, his lookouts spotted gunfire flashes, so he knew where their enemy lay. And once again, the spartan night battle-training that Admiral Yamamoto had forced upon the Japanese Combined Fleet came into play. It was to decide the course of this action much more than did the Americans' superior radar.

Tanaka's chief of staff signaled for a mass torpedo attack by the Japanese destroyers. The destroyer *Takanami* fired torpedoes and then turned sharply to the right. She was nearest to the Americans, and the radar screens had her. The American ships began firing on her, and she replied with her own guns. But she was the cynosure of all radar that night, and in a few minutes she was reduced to a wreck.

The flagship *Naganami* also fired torpedoes. The *Makinami*, next in line, led the supply destroyers (with their single torpedoes in each tube) to drop their drums of supply, and then turned to the battle.

Despite the surprise and their preoccupation with the unloading of the supply drums, the Japanese destroyers managed to fire more than twenty torpedoes in the first few moments of the battle. When the Japanese ships began to maneuver, the shooting became harder for the Americans because their highly vaunted radar did not always perform to specifications. The Americans made the mistake of zeroing in on the wreckage of the *Takanami*, for example, when shooting at other targets would have been much more profitable.

The Japanese were at first not firing their guns, but only their torpedes. Even when the Japanese did fire, they used flashless powder, giving the Americans no aiming points.

In the beginning the action seemed to be all American. The *Takanami* blazed and exploded, to the cheers of the American sailors. But just before 11:30, as the *Minneapolis* was firing her ninth salvo (probably at the *Takanami*), two Japanese torpedoes struck her, breaking loose sixty feet of the bow, and causing her to list sharply to port. Next, a torpedo hit the cruiser *New Orleans*, blowing off the whole forward part of the ship. The third American ship to be hit was the *Pensacola*, struck below the mainmast on the port side. That blow flooded the after engine room, and put three gun turrets out of action. Speed was cut to 8 knots, and the ship moved out of the action toward Tulagi. The *Northampton* was next. Her captain was maneuvering to avoid torpedoes, but the destroyer *Oyashio* fired eight torpeodes and two of them connected. The *Northampton*'s after engine room became an aquarium, the ship listed to port, and the after end of the ship flared up in yellow flame. Swiftly she went dead in the water.

The Japanese, having thrown their cargo over, and having rescued some survivors from the *Takanami*, hurried to get clear of Ironbottom Sound, and by 1:30 in the morning were out of harm's way. They pulled into Shortlands Harbor the next morning before noon, claiming to have sunk a battleship and two cruisers and to have damaged four other warships. That was nonsense, of course. Nevertheless, the Japanese *had* done a remarkable job on the American cruiser force.

The Americans spent most of the rest of the night fruitlessly searching for the enemy and rescuing survivors of the battered American ships. The *Minneapolis* made it to Tulagi. The *New Orleans*, with 120 feet of her bow missing and many dead and wounded, also made it to Tulagi a day later. So did the *Pensacola*, but the *Northampton* did not. She struggled for life in the early hours of the morning, and then finally sank, leaving men struggling in the water. Remarkably, 773 of the crew of 831 officers and men were rescued from the water.

The damage to the American vessels was so serious that the *Minneapolis* and the *New Orleans* had to go back to the American coast for repair. The *Pensacola* went to Pearl Harbor. They were all out of action for many months.

So the battle of Tassafaronga was very definitely a Japanese victory, a victory of training and experience over a superior physical force with superior technology. And the fact was that the American marksmanship, even with radar, was not impressive, while the Japanese marksmanship, even with no impressive technology, was superb. But so high was the standard of Japanese seamanship and gunnery that Admiral Yamamoto found nothing particularly remarkable in the victory. His major concern at that time was, and continued to be, Admiral Tanaka's effectiveness in supplying the Japanese troops on Guadalcanal. For Yamamoto knew very well that he could win every naval engagement and still the Japanese would lose Guadalcanal unless they could capture Henderson Field and regain air superiority in the southern Solomons.

CHAPTER FOURTEEN

The End on Guadalcanal

On December 1, the Japanese supply situation on Guadalcanal was serious. By December 15, it was desperate, and even coconuts were in short supply. Admiral Tanaka's supply ships came down every four or five days, but they could not carry enough to feed all the troops. The submarine supply service was interdicted from time to time by the growing number of PT Boats at Tulagi.

On December 3 Admiral Tanaka brought ten destroyers down to Guadalcanal. They discharged their cargo and ran back to the Shortlands. The Americans attacked from the air and put a bomb into the destroyer *Makinami*, but the convoy had air cover and so the American attack was blunted.

On December 7 the Tanaka force came again with eleven destroyers, but the *Nowacki* was "near-missed" by a bomb that blew in her engine room plating and killed seventeen men. Still the supplies got off, but how many drums were carried out to sea by tide and winds is not known. In any case, the supplies were not adequate for the men ashore and they slowly starved.

At Rabaul General Imamura spoke of putting 50,000 men on the island. He had them at Rabaul, but getting them from Rabaul to Guadalcanal was an impossible task as the Cactus Air Force continued to grow. Even though Japan maintained control of the sea, it did not have control of the waters around Guadalcanal at night. The submarine *I-3* came in with a load of supplies on December 9 and was preparing to discharge them when she was attacked by *PT-59* and sunk.

On December 11 Tanaka was back again, his destroyers having come unscathed through an air attack off New Georgia. But the PT boats got at him, sinking the destroyer *Teruzuki* and frustrating the attempt to land the supplies by buzzing around the convoy like angry bees.

The Americans maintained a PT boat patrol between Kokumbona and Cape Esperance, and every night had four boats at the ready in Tulagi harbor. The result was the more and more hasty jettisoning of supplies by the "Tokyo Express," with the further result that more and more drums never got close enough to shore for recovery by the troops.

In December, preparing for the new assault on Guadalcanal, the Japanese built up an airfield in southern New Georgia Island, ten miles north of Rendova, which was to be the point of air attack on Henderson Field, 175 miles to the south. The place was a prewar coconut plantation at Munda. The job was begun under concealment by very clever camouflage, leaving the coconut trees standing as long as possible, and when they had to be removed, laying palm fronds on overhead wires, to simulate coconut palms. This device fooled the Allied airmen who came snooping, but was ultimately uncovered by aerial photographs that showed a 2000-foot runway and antiaircraft gun emplacements all around the field.

The field was completed in the first week of December, and it then became the focal point for a series of air attacks day and night. But the Japanese continued to work and by mid-December were flying aircraft from the field to engage the Cactus Air Force on more equal terms. The Japanese were also staging supplies into Guadalcanal by barge from New Georgia, but these barges, too, became a focal point for attack, and many of them were lost. Because of a shortage of destroyers, the Tanaka run was curtailed at the end of December. At that same time Imperial General Headquarters in Tokyo came to the conclusion that the supply situation was so desperate on Guadalcanal that the island would have to be evacuated, rather than reinforced. New

Guinea was to become the primary target of conquest, with Guadalcanal to follow after Port Moresby had been occupied. So the Japanese concentrated on building up New Georgia.

Rabaul became busier than ever as the Japanese concentrated supplies and men there for shipment to New Guinea and the central Solomons. On New Year's Eve, 1942, aerial photos of Simpson Harbor at Rabaul showed a hundred ships swinging at anchor.

Transports and cargo vessels were still being used to supply New Georgia and New Guinea, but not Guadalcanal. The Cactus Air Force was too fearsome, the distance for escorting planes too great, and the Allied buildup in the Guadalcanal area too strong. For example, on January 2, the "Tokyo Express" came down, ten destroyers strong, to try to deliver supplies to the beleaguered troops of General Hyukatake. They were attacked en route by B-17s, which scored some near misses. Off Guadalcanal they were attacked by navy dive-bombers, one of which put a bomb so close to the destroyer *Suzukaze* that it caused her to drop out of formation, taking another destroyer out for escort. They were then attacked by PT boats, which failed to sink any ships, but were able to sink the supply drums left behind, which made the supply mission a total failure. Now in great number, the PT boats had become the primary problem for the supply missions. With these continuous failures the Japanese became more and more worried. They tried air-dropping bundles of supply, but most of the drops fell into deep jungle and were lost.

The Americans' days of desperation were well behind them. Soon General Patch would have 35,000 troops; the Americans continued their buildup on Guadalcanal. But the army's conduct of the war was inept to say the least. Early in December General Sebree decided to take Mt. Austin, which was occupied by a small but well-dug-in force of Japanese—about three-hundred men. He thought a company should be able to do the job. It was the same sort of mistake that the Japanese had made when they sent Colonel Ichiki to the island to route the First Marine Division with a thousand men. In the event, the company became a battalion, and the commander then asked for another battalion in support, and after three weeks of launching ineffectual attacks supported by air strikes and artillery, they gave up. The two battalions had suffered 182 battle casualties and nearly that number had come down with malaria and/or dysentery. The whole assault had been a fiasco, and only a half a dozen Japanese had been killed.

In Tokyo a debate had begun in December about Guadalcanal. Emissaries from the Imperial General Headquarters had come to Guadalcanal, to Rabaul, and to Truk to investigate, and had returned to Tokyo with the information that the struggle to resupply Guadalcanal under present conditions was proving very expensive in ships and aircraft that could be better employed elsewhere. So the decision was made to hang Guadalcanal on a limb, move the troops out, and come back later, when the capture of New Guinea had loosened the Allied hold on the area. Admiral Yamamoto agreed with this view, because the disastrous land campaign of the army had caused him so much trouble. The failure of the navy resupply campaign had also cost Admiral Tanaka his job. He had been relieved by Yamamoto for his "failure" and would spend the rest of the war as commander of the Japanese naval base at Rangoon.

At Rabaul Admiral Jinichi Kusaka and General Imamura disagreed with the IGHQ; they believed Tokyo should send the resources to recapture Guadalcanal immediately and not wait for developments. They held the traditional view that the Japanese army and navy were unbeatable. They felt that if the island were to be abandoned to the enemy, the Allies would continue to expand operations in the Solomons and threaten the Japanese hold on Rabaul itself. But in Tokyo the army and navy high commands were counting the cost and they had other ideas.

These ideas were enhanced by the Japanese observation that the Americans were building up their forces in the South Pacific—which indeed they were, on the sea as well as in the air and on land.

On December 31, General Sugiyama, chief of staff of the Imperial Army, and Admiral Osami Nagano, chief of staff of the navy, went to the Imperial Palace to discuss the situation on Guadalcanal with Emperor Hirohito. He already knew that the Guadalcanal campaign had gone very badly. In spite of the almost continuous victories of the Japanese navy, the army had been unable to capture the airfield. So it was really no surprise to the emperor when they suggested that the assault on Guadalcanal be "temporarily" abandoned in favor of a much larger assault on New Guinea. He agreed.

The American army commander, General Patch, decided to start a new offensive on Guadalcanal in January, and the force was augmented to about 40,000 men, the greatest element being the Twenty-fourth Army Corps. The attack was begun in force in the second week of January. General Hyukatake and the men on Guadalcanal did not want to give up, but the reinforcement program had come a cropper and the emperor had acceded to the army-navy request to get out.

On Guadalcanal the Japanese fought hard and conducted a series of raids against Henderson Field and other points. The Americans brought in another division, the Twenty-fifth, and by the end of January had 50,000 men on the island. In mid-January the Japanese destroyer force brought down a six-hundred man unit which would cover the Japanese army withdrawal from Guadalcanal.

By this time Admiral Halsey, who had just been promoted to full admiral, had a real admiral's command. The carrier *Saratoga* had been sent back to the South Pacific and the *Enterprise* was still there. Rear Admiral Walden Lee Ainsworth had four light cruisers and four destroyers. Rear Admiral Lee had the battleship force, which had lost the damaged *South Dakota*, but gained the new *North Carolina* and *Indiana* to sail with the *Washington*. And Rear Admiral Robert Giffen had just brought a new task force—Task Force 18—to the South Pacific. This untried admiral had two escort carriers, the *Chenango* and the *Suwannee*, three cruisers, three light cruisers, and eight destroyers under his command. His force was experimental, and not very intelligently so. Because the little carriers could make only 18 knots, while the cruisers could make 30. Admiral Giffen called the "jeep" carriers "my ball and chain."

The Americans were bringing in thousands of troops in four big transports at the end of January, preparing for the big push to oust the Japanese. Halsey wanted to assure their safety, so he ordered Admiral Giffen to meet the transports and the destroyer escort near Lunga. To do this, Giffen set sail on the afternoon of January 29, but he had to leave behind his escort carriers so that he could push forward at 24 knots, six knots faster than the escort carriers' top speed. The little carriers kept a combat air patrol over the cruiser force all that day, however, even though they lagged far behind themselves.

The Japanese were well aware of the coming of the American force because they had assembled several submarines in the Guadalcanal area in preparation for their destroyer evacuation of the island, which would begin in a few days. The submarines reported on the Giffen task force, and word reached Munda airfield, where a large number of Japanese aircraft had now been moved.

As dusk fell on January 29, thirty-one Japanese bombers were in the air, headed for the Giffen force. They skirted around the American vessels by flying to the south, where they would not be silhouetted against the evening sky, and a handful of them made an attack, narrowly missing the cruiser *Chicago* and strafing several ships. One twin-engine bomber was shot down.

So relaxed was Admiral Giffen that his ships were not all at general quarters for this attack, and that hampered the defenses more than a little bit. He also thought that it was all over when the first flight of bombers passed away. How wrong he was; at dark Japanese floatplanes began dropping flares around the task force, indicating the type of ship, the course and speed, and the bombers came in again.

This time they put two torpedoes into the *Chicago*, which went dead in the water. The *Louisville* took her in tow, and later the tow was transferred to the fleet tug *Navajo*. The task force changed course and in the darkness the Japanese bomber force lost track of the American ships, so they were safe for the night.

At Noumea Admiral Halsey ordered the two little carriers to speed to the scene and put up combat air patrol in the morning over the cruiser force, and he also ordered the *Enterprise* to do the same. But that day the Japanese were out looking again and they found the task force, which had left the wounded *Chicago* behind with four destroyers. Just before four o'clock in the afternoon, a dozen Japanese torpedo bombers attacked. Three of them were shot down right away by planes from the *Enterprise*, but the other nine attacked. Seven of these were also shot down by aircraft and antiaircraft fire, but the bomber force put four more torpedoes into the *Chicago*, sinking her, and one torpedo into the destroyer *La Vallette*, making her inoperable. She was saved by being towed back to Noumea by the tug *Navajo*, and 1049 survivors of the *Chicago* were also rescued from the water.

Meanwhile, the four big transports, without the cruiser force support, reached Guadalcanal and unloaded without a hitch. The last naval action of the struggle for Guadalcanal thus ended.

On the night of February 1 the Japanese began Operation KE, the evacuation of Guadalcanal, supported by all the air power that could be brought down from Rabaul. The evacuation was carried out with great secrecy and effectiveness. The American coast watchers and air observers knew that something was going on, but they concluded that the Japanese were building up their Guadalcanal force. That night two American destroyers were escorting three LCTs south of Savo Island when they ran afoul of Japanese air cover for the evacuation. The destroyer *DeHaven* was sunk, and the *Nicholas* was damaged by bombs.

That night twenty Japanese destroyers came down the Slot and were attacked by planes from Henderson Field. But their Zero escort shot down four American planes, and only one Japanese destroyer the *Makinami*, was damaged. Later that night the destroyer *Makigumo* ran into an American mine and had to be scuttled. PT boats attacked the Japanese ships but did no damage. The destroyer picked up about a third of the Japanese survivors and made off for the north without further incident until the next morning, when the ships were attacked, but not damaged, by planes from Henderson Field.

On Guadalcanal, the Americans, deeply involved in their "offensive," did not even suspect what was happening, even when, without any trouble at all, they captured the base at Tassafaronga, only to find it completely abandoned. They reasoned that the Japanese had withdrawn to a consolidated position to start another attack.

On February 4, the Japanese destroyers were back to pick up another group of the Seventeenth Army—a cruiser and twenty-two destroyers. And on February 17 the navy sent in its last rescue mission, taking off the remainder of the Seventeenth Army, a total of almost 12,000 men—all that remained of the more than 25,000 who had come to the island to recapture it for Japan. The Americans were a week in discovering that there were no more Japanese on the island, so skillfully was it done. In the end, Admiral Nimitz praised his enemies for having carried out the most stunning evacuation in military history.

CHAPTER FIFTEEN

The Submarines

Admiral Yamamoto had been waiting since Midway for the opportunity to engage the major elements of the American fleet and win a "decisive victory" at sea. It was his theory that the only way Japan could disengage herself from the war the generals had gotten her into was to win big enough somewhere to put the Americans off balance—then to quickly talk peace.

But by the beginning of 1943 the opportunity was lost. The American naval buildup program was going full blast; the new battleships, the new cruisers, and the new escort carriers that appeared in the South Pacific were proof of it. Still another aspect of the American might was making itself felt in the South Pacific that winter: the increasing effectiveness of the American submarines. One reason the Japanese could not engage after the battle of Guadalcanal was the fuel shortage that had caused Tokyo to limit Admiral Yamamoto's fuel supplies. The reason that Admiral Kondo's big surface fleet was milling about Ontong, Java, was to remain near Japan's only natural oil supply in the Dutch East Indies. And by 1943 that oil supply was being sharply cut by the depradations of American submarines.

The American submarine force had started out slow. Before the war broke out, submarines in the Pacific were stationed in two areas outside the continental United States: in Pearl Harbor, the base of the American Pacific Fleet, and in Manila Bay, the base of the U.S. Asiatic Fleet. When war broke out, patrols from both bases began to move into the waters controlled by Japan.

Asiatic Fleet submarines were not at first very effective. Most of them were the old S boats, called "pigboats," the leftovers from a previous war. They were slow and small and they had torpedo troubles. The magnetic exploders of the torpedoes often did not function and the torpedoes sometimes ran too deep and thus went under the target ships.

Captain John Wilkes was the commander of submarines in the Asiatic Fleet. As the war progressed he moved over to the tunnels of Corregidor, where he operated until December 31, when he realized that his position there was untenable. At that point he had ten submarines and accompanying shore personnel. He divided the specialists into two parts: half, under Captain James Fife, were sent to Darwin to establish a submarine base that would be under the general command of General Douglas MacArthur when he got to Australia. The other half left for Surabaya, in Java, to join Admiral Thomas C. Hart and the remnants of the Asiatic Fleet in their struggle to fend off the Japanese in the Dutch East Indies.

By March, the Allies had realized that the Java campaign was lost. Captain Wilkes moved the submarine tender *Holland* down to the south coast of Java, and then, in March, when the Battle of the Java Sea was lost, he moved the command to Western Australia, at Fremantle. In the spring of 1942, Captain Ralph Christie was sent out to Brisbane to command a group of the old S boats, that had been provided to augment the Far Eastern submarine force. So there were three separate submarine commands operating out of Australia: Wilkes's at Fremantle, Fife's at Darwin, and Christie's at Brisbane. Soon Captain Wilkes was sent home to command a cruiser, and Captain Charles A. Lockwood was brought from London to take command at Fremantle. He was soon promoted to rear admiral and became the senior submarine commander in the South Pacific.

Life was made more complicated for the submarine force in July 1942, when Rear Admiral Arthur S. Carpender, a spit-and-polish officer, was designated commander of American naval forces in Australia. This had been done as a sop to General MacArthur, who was demanding a naval force of his own. The navy could not give him ships other than submarines, but they could give him a commander. So Admiral Carpender took over the shadow command, and began making life miserable for the submarines because he had nothing much else to do.

Admiral Lockwood's submarine command included all of the Dutch East Indies and their adjacent waters, the Philippines, and the coast of Indo-China. The distances were so great that sometimes the submarines ran low on fuel before they had spent their torpedoes, which was a great waste. So, in the fall of 1942, a new operating base was set up at Exmouth Gulf, on the north side of Australia, 750 miles closer to the scene of the action than Fremantle. With this, the submarines, became more effective. By now, Lockwood had twenty submarines.

At the time of the marine invasion of Guadalcanal, Captain Christie's S-boat force was operating out of Brisbane, and his activity was closely linked to General MacArthur's New Guinea campaign. Within a few hours of the invasion, the American *S-44* sank the Japanese cruiser *Kako*, the first major warship of Japan to be sunk by an American submarine in the Pacific war.

By fall the American submarines from Pearl Harbor were ranging around the Japanese islands, taking a good toll of tankers and merchant ships. But in the South Pacific, the Japanese submarines were doing a much better job of fighting the battle of Guadalcanal than were the American submarines. The reason lay primarily in their different philosophies of submarine usage. The Japanese used their submarines as part of the fleet, not as commerce destroyers. And so the Japanese submarines were always on the prowl around Guadalcanal. At the height of the campaign they had sunk the carrier *Wasp* and several destroyers, damaged the battleship *North Carolina* and a number of supply ships, hit the cruiser *Chester* and sent her back to the U.S. for repairs. They had also used midget submarines for an attack on Sydney harbor, and off Guadalcanal to torpedo the supply ship *Majaba*. An I boat had sunk the cruiser *Juneau*. Until they were diverted to supply missions (when the Japanese destroyers failed to give sufficient help to the men of Guadalcancal), the Japanese submarines had run up an impressive record of sinking warships.

The major American submarine contribution at Guadalcanal was by the *Amberjack*. At the height of the struggle for air supremacy on Guadalcanal, the *Amberjack* was commandeered by Admiral Halsey and made to carry 9000 gallons of aviation gas, fifteen pilots, and a load of bombs to Guadalcanal.

In the fall of 1942 the American submarines in Australia suffered from a torpedo shortage, and Admiral Lockwood put his skippers on rations—twenty torpedo, per patrol instead of twenty-four. Finally the shortage grew so severe that Lockwood cut the torpedo ration to eight per ship.

But by the end of 1942, the United States was producing many new fleet-class submarines, and the torpedo situation was improving. The economic blockade of Japan was really about to begin on an organized basis. To date, American submarines in the Pacific had sunk only about one-sixth the number of ships that the German U-boats had sunk in the Atlantic and adjacent waters. They had sunk 725,000 tons of Japanese shipping, but the Japanese had built 625,000 tons during the same time, so the results were not very impressive. But as 1943 began, all that changed. The Americans now had a force of eighty submarines in the Pacific, a 40-percent increase over the last few months. Captain Fife began concentrating his submarine activity around Guadalcanal and the new Japanese base on New Georgia.

The submarine command changed drastically that winter. Admiral Robert English, the commander of Pacific Fleet submarines, was killed in a plane crash, and Admiral Lockwood succeeded him at Pearl Harbor. Captain Fife continued in Darwin, and Captain Christie was promoted to Rear Admiral, succeeding Admiral Lockwood at Fremantle. But the real change was the increase of submarine activity in the area, and the increased effectiveness of that activity.

The submarine *Growler* left Brisbane on New Year's Day 1943, and in short order sank two Japanese troop transports, the *Chifuku Maru* and the *Miyodono Maru*, and damaged another transport. Coming atop the losses of the autumn at Guadalcanal this was very serious news for the Japanese army.

In January, the *Wahoo* was sent to Wewak (at the time, the Americans did not even know where it was) and found elements of the Japanese fleet there. Captain Dudley Morton sank a destroyer there and torpedoed four merchant vessels, one of which was loaded with Japanese troops.

The exploits of the *Wahoo* and several other submarines caused the Japanese to tighten their antisubmarine warfare campaign, and also to divert more destroyers from fleet work to escort of convoys carrying men and supplies to the South Pacific and oil to Japan. So the balance of submarine power in the South Pacific began to shift. By the spring of 1943 the Japanese submarine force was definitely on the defensive.

CHAPTER SIXTEEN

"Stop the Enemy..."

On the last day of 1942, when General Sugiyama and Admiral Nagano went with General Tojo, the prime minister, to call on Emperor Hirohito and inform him that the war situation in the Pacific dictated the withdrawal of Japanese troops for the moment, the emperor had a question for them.

"What do you intend to do next?"

The answer: "Stop the enemy's westward movement."

The subsidiary answer, explained most apologetically, was that Japan would first stop the enemy's westward movement, then recapture Guadalcanal and capture British New Guinea almost simultaneously. This would put the Japanese war plan back on the track that would lead to the ultimate conquest of Australia and the protection of the far-flung new empire.

Already, said Admiral Nagano, the Japanese navy and army in cooperation were developing air bases on Munda and Kolombangara, from which they intended to pulverize Guadalcanal from the air. When they were ready, the first move would be to launch an all-out air offensive to break Allied air power over Guadalcanal. They would reinforce Japanese troops on New Guinea, take Port Moresby, and reinvade Guadalcanal. This operation would be called the I Operation.

In the revised war plan established at the end of 1942,

the central Solomons became the Japanese defense line. The navy was to have the responsibility for defending New Georgia, Vella Lavella, Kolombangara, and Bougainville islands, and the army would *take* the responsibility for capture of Port Moresby and capturing the southern half of New Guinea.

The Americans were totally surprised by the Japanese evacuation of Guadalcanal in the first days of February 1942, and they were not prepared to exploit that change. They had neither the ships, the men, nor the plan for future action. Admiral Nimitz had come to the South Pacific in January and being Nimitz, was always thinking ahead. He told Halsey at that time that, as soon as Guadalcanal was secured, he wanted to take the Russell Islands, the next step in the northward flow of the Solomons chain, located just thirty miles from Cape Esperance on Guadalcanal. In January the Americans estimated that the Japanese had 5000 troops in the Russells and that dislodging them would be a difficult operation—about double the scale of the Tulagi invasion of August. As soon as Admiral Halsey learned that the Japanese had evacuated Guadalcanal, then, on February 7, 1943, he ordered the amphibious attack on the Russells, just to keep moving.

Rear Admiral Richmond Kelly Turner came down to Koli Point, Guadalcanal, and worked out the invasion of the Russells. It would be done with minimal naval forces, as much air support as Henderson Field could manage, and small landing craft since the distances were so short. The troops would be a mixed contingent of army, navy and marines.

The composition of the force indicated how hard up the Americans were just then for troops to undertake the missions of this fast-moving war. To the Russells were assigned:

Part of the Forty-third U.S. Army Infantry Division

One-third of the Eleventh Marine Defense Battalion

The Tenth Marine Defense Battalion

The Third Marine Raider Battalion

Part of the Thirty-fifth Naval Construction Battalion

A naval boat pool

Eight PT Boats

Artillery batteries borrowed from everywhere

A reserve regiment of one regimental combat team, not named, to come from the Twenty-fourth U.S. Army Corps.

A few hours before the kickoff of the invasion, Admiral Turner was informed that the Japanese had abandoned the Russells in the evacuation of Guadalcanal. But that did not make any difference. The plans were made and they would be carried out to give amphibious command practice for the future.

The American troops were brought down to Guadalcanal by five big military transports escorted by six destroyers. They were attacked on the night of February 17 by a flight of twin-engine Japanese bombers carrying torpedoes, but the convoy commander acted with great skill and the destroyers fought valiantly with their antiaircraft guns. The Japanese planes were either driven off or destroyed without damage to the convoy.

The invasion of the Russell Islands itself, was completely anticlimactic. The convoy of small vessels left Guadalcanal on February 20 and steamed across the water without incident. At dawn they reached the Russells, and it was simply a question of going ashore. No shooting, no blood, no enemy. During the next week 9000 men went ashore to begin construction of an air field and facilities for PT boats.

But the Japanese were not far away. They were building up their forces on Kolombangara Island and on New Georgia, across Kula Gulf. At this point Admiral Yamamoto could still attack Guadalcanal, and more successfully than ever, staging planes down from Rabaul to Buka Island at the tip of Bougainville, or to Kahili, near Buin at the southern end of Bougainville, or to Ballale, Vila, and thence to the new base at Munda on New Georgia. That was the most dangerous of all to the Americans at Henderson Field. But the problem for the Japanese in the winter months of 1943 was the enormous Allied buildup, particularly in the air. Once the Allied air forces had been vastly inferior to that of their enemy; now they were superior, and several more landing strips were added at Guadalcanal, including one at Koli Point. Admiral Halsey now had more than three-hundred aircraft on Guadalcanal, including bombers, fighters, and the night-fighter Black Cats.

These days—or nights—the Japanese were doing in the central Solomons what they had done earlier at Guadalcanal, running night supply missions. On February 19 the transport *Yokuwaru Maru* ran a gauntlet of American fighter planes, but arrived and discharged most of its cargo safely and went back to Rabaul without further incident.

The American buildup of Guadalcanal and the occupation of the Russells caused the Japanese many new problems in resupply. Their answer was to concentrate their efforts during the ten days of the dark of the moon. That, said the Japanese navy, would be the time when they would run the resupply missions. When the army objected to this program, the navy informed them about the great buildup of Henderson Field, and warned that if the army intended to hold its positions on New Georgia and Kolombangara it would have to supply more men. The army was very reluctant to do so, considering this to be navy territory, but the navy did not have the personnel to man the two big islands. So, reluctantly, General Imamura agreed to build up his forces, and did increase the garrisons of the two islands to about ten thousand men.

These Japanese reinforcements were brought in by transports. On February 27 the *Kirikawa Maru* made the run down from Rabaul, escorted by a minesweeper and a sub-chaser. At the Kolombangara anchorage the ships were attacked by American planes, but Zeroes from Rabaul had been sent down, and they drove the Americans away. On the return voyage early in March, the *Kirikawa Maru* was found by more of the ranging American bombers, and this time she was sunk. The heavy loss of transports disturbed the Japanese more than a little bit, and the Americans constantly stepped up their level of activity.

On the night of March 5, four American destroyers came down to do to the Japanese what the Japanese had done to them for so long on Guadalcanal: bombard their airfield at Munda. They fired 1600 rounds of five-inch ammunition at the airfield that night, and did considerable damage to planes and facilities. But as with Henderson Field, Munda was in operation again the next day.

The next night Rear Admiral A. S. Merrill took three cruisers and three destroyers to bombard Vila airfield on Kolombangara. While Admiral Merrill was at sea he got a message from Guadalcanal alerting him to the coming that night of a two-destroyer resupply mission to Vila. The destroyers *Murasame* and *Minegumo* were on their way. They steamed down past Vella Lavella Island into Blackett Strait, and arrived at Vila before midnight. They unloaded their cargoes successfully onto barges that went ashore; then the two Japanese destroyers headed back for Rabaul. But instead of retracing their steps, the commander chose to take a shortcut through Kula Gulf to the Shortlands, and on the way ran smack into Admiral Merrill's force. By this time the Americans had most of their radar problems solved and were able to use the device successfully. They found the Japanese ships with radar and attacked. The cruisers used their guns, the destroyers, used their torpedoes, and they sank both Japanese ships in short order. The destroyer *Waller* accounted for one of the enemy ships with at least one of the five torpedoes she fired.

For the Americans it was a clean, clear-cut victory with no fumbling, for almost the first time in the South Pacific campaign. The American destroyer men, in particular, had begun this war vastly inferior in training to the enemy's, but now they were beginning to catch up. And the improvements in the American radar use were spectacular. From now on radar would play a far more important part in Japanese-American battles than it had done before.

CHAPTER SEVENTEEN

The Struggle for Air Power

Admirals Halsey and Yamamoto could agree on one aspect of strategy in the South Pacific: he who controlled the air would also control the sea. Both sides spent the early weeks of 1943 trying to build up their air strength for coming operations. The new airstrips that suddenly began appearing in the Central Solomons represented Yamamoto's efforts. So did his unremitting calls on Tokyo for a greater share in aircraft production for the navy because of the extension of its mission in the South and Southwest Pacific. The pleas fell on deaf ears; the generals were not about to give up any of their precious aircraft, although they did not seem to know what to do with them in the Pacific islands. The fact was that General Tojo had never really been convinced that the Allies had staying power in the Pacific. Even in the winter of 1943 he still believed that if he could bring Chiang Kai-shek to terms in China, the Pacific war would end because the Allies would be sick of it and ready to give Japan her way in Asia.

As for the Americans, they were introducing major improvements in their air power program. Quietly, without enough fanfare to alert the Japanese at Rabaul, Lieutenant General George F. Kenney was building up the Fifth Air

Force in Australia. The first P-38s arrived in September 1942, though they were not operational until December. The force of medium attack-planes—A-20s, B-25s, and B-26s—was steadily building, and in January they stepped up the strength of their attacks on Rabaul.

At Noumea, Admiral Halsey was also fighting for more air power. The Wildcat fighter was being replaced by the F6F Hellcat and the gull-winged F4U, which had twice the range of the Hellcat. The B-24 Liberator was proving to be remarkably adaptable to South Pacific work against ships and shore installations, and could carry more bombs than the B-17. The commander of land-based air in the South Pacific was Vice Admiral Aubrey W. Fitch, a real expert in his job, and there was no more fumbling in the use of search and reconnaissance planes.

On December 24, 1942, Japanese Vice Admiral Kusaka, commander of the Eleventh Air Fleet at Rabaul, was appointed commander of the Southeast Area Fleet, which made him responsible for all naval activity in the Bismarck, Solomon, and New Guinea areas. He took on the new Munda strip and several others and strengthened the forces at Rabaul, which had recently undergone several heavy American air attacks from the Australian Fifth Air Force in Australia.

But during the first two months of 1943, there was no major move by either side. General Tojo was concentrating his efforts on China. The American navy would have liked to launch a direct attack on the Bonin Islands, about five hundred miles from Tokyo, but the invasion of North Africa had bogged down, and the American promise that Hitler would be fought first had to be honored. The coming of ships and planes to the Pacific was therefore delayed. Admiral Nimitz did not want to get into a major fleet battle with Admiral Yamamoto, until he had the new *Essex*-class carriers, which would be available, it was said, around the middle of 1943. So, in essence, both sides were on "hold" and told to make the most of their resources and do the best they could.

To prepare, the U.S. Navy made some administrative changes, creating three fleets in the Pacific: the Third Fleet, which was Admiral Halsey's; the Fifth Fleet, which was

Vice Admiral Raymond Spruance's, and the Seventh Fleet, which soon became Admiral Thomas C. Kinkaid's.

At the end of February, the Japanese decided to make a major effort to strengthen their forces in New Guinea and sent a large convoy of troops and supply out into the Bismarck Sea. It was ambushed by Lieutenant General Kenney's Fifth Air Force and virtually destroyed, shaking the Japanese establishment at Rabaul to the bottom of their boots.*

The result of the Battle the Bismarck Sea was recognition by Japan's Imperial General Headquarters that air power was the single biggest factor in the southern seas equation. Admiral Yamamoto had spoken earlier of making a serious drive to knock out growing Allied air power in the Solomons and New Guinea. But during January and February nothing had been done; he had scarcely received enough aircraft to maintain a limited schedule of operations.

In March, when Japanese aircraft production would hit five hundred planes a month, Yamamoto was finally given the go-ahead for Operation I, the move to wreck the Allied air power. Admiral Yamamoto made preparations to move down to Rabaul from the flagship at Truk for the campaign. He had been ordered to concentrate the air activity against the MacArthur forces in New Guinea, but he insisted that to do so would be to encourage the Allies to attack in the Solomons. So he split the operation into two parts, one directed against Guadalcanal and the Russell Islands, and the other against New Guinea.

Because Tokyo had still not provided enough aircraft to carry out the mission, Yamamoto was forced to denude his aircraft carriers to obtain enough skilled air crews and planes. Altogether about three hundred aircraft were first concentrated at Rabaul, and then moved around to airfields at Buka, Kahili, and Ballale to set up the attacks.

The air action of April 1, which presaged Operation I, indicated the kind of problem that Yamamoto now faced. He sent down sixty fighters to Guadalcanal on a sweep; over

---

*The story of the Battle of the Bismarck Sea is essentially a part of the battle for New Guinea, and I have dealt with it in detail in *The Jungles of New Guinea*, Volume 4 in this series of Pacific war histories.

Guadalcanal, they were intercepted by forty-one American fighters including the F-4Us and the P-38 Interceptor fighters. Eighteen Japanese planes were shot down, while only six American planes fell. Six months earlier the ratio might have been the reverse. But in the past half year the Americans had improved their aircraft remarkably, and their pilots were gaining ever more skill, while the ranks of Japanese naval pilots were being winnowed by attrition. There was no rotation in the Japanese navy; a man went to his assigned squadron and remained there until it was moved or he was dead. But by the spring of 1943, most of the pilots of the Eleventh Air Fleet were replacements, and replacements of replacements, and so were some of the carrier pilots lent for the occasion.

On April 3 Admiral Yamamoto and his staff flew down to Rabaul and broke out the admiral's flag over the Southeast Area Fleet office. Yamamoto did not need to come down, but he felt that his airmen should have all the encouragement he could give them in what he knew was a most difficult task.

On April 4 Admiral Yamamoto went by car to the Rabaul airfield, where the 204th Air Group was stationed, and wearing white gloves and a snow-white uniform covered with medals, he led a celebration of obeisance to the emperor and then made a little speech about Operation I. The purpose of the action was to destroy the enemy's air power and sea power in all the region, he said. And if the men thought it was difficult, let them also remember that the Allied airmen were suffering as much as they.

The weather at Rabaul was stormy that day, so operations had to be postponed. The weather remained so bad that operations could not be resumed until the morning of April 7. That day—fortuitously, as it appeared to Yamamoto—came a report of a big Allied naval force clustered around Guadalcanal. It was just the sort of concentration Yamamoto had hoped to find—five cruisers, ten destroyers, and ten transports.

On this X-day the mission was led by Captain Miyano, the commander of the 204th Air Group, who so obviously did not expect to return that he did not even wear his parachute. He led 157 fighters and sixty-seven bombers to

Guadalcanal that day. Admiral Yamamoto stood on the side of the field waving his admiral's cap as the planes took off. He did not leave until the last aircraft was gone.

The planes flew down to Buin, where some peeled off and waited for a flight of dive-bombers. The rest went on to Buka to refuel. This was a sign of the new offensive—no longer would they have to make that gruelling nonstop flight to Guadalcanal, but could stop at Buka and at Munda, which was within easy fighting distance of the southern island.

The Japanese that morning counted fourteen transports and a naval task force, but Admiral Ainsworth had moved his cruisers to safer waters in the south. Still, Ironbottom Sound was filled with ships, destroyers, transports, tankers, and work ships. And across on the Tulagi side there was the new PT boat base with a tender, several LCTs, several visiting New Zealand warships, and seven small transports.

Seventy-six fighters were sent up from Henderson Field to stop the Japanese. The fighting went on for hours, and at the end of it the Japanese claimed ten transports sunk, a cruiser and a destroyer sunk, and three other transports damaged. They also claimed to have shot down forty-one enemy fighters and damaged another thirty-one, with Japanese losses of twelve fighters and nine bombers.

The Americans counted:

One New Zealand corvette, the *Moa*, sunk

One American destroyer, the *Aaron Ward*, sunk

One U.S. tanker, the *Kanawha*, sunk

Three ships damaged by near misses.

The Americans claimed to have shot down one hundred Japanese planes with a loss of only seven American fighters.

The encounter delayed the American plans and also caused the command at Guadalcanal to go slow, anticipating further attacks. But the Japanese considered the Solomons and New Guinea a part of the same operation and so the next strike came against Oro Bay, where cargo ships were unloading supplies for the Allied air bases at Dobodura.

It came on April 11, and was called Y–2. Shortly after noon a Japanese force of twenty-one bombers and seventy-one Zeroes appeared, virtually without warning, over the New Guinea port. Fifty Allied fighters came up from Dobodura and the Zeroes attacked them to prevent destruction of their bombers. The Japanese claimed to have sunk three transports and a destroyer, with a loss of two fighters and four bombers. The Americans claimed to have shot down six enemy planes, which tallied with the Japanese version for a change, but to have lost no planes themselves, while the Japanese said they had shot down twenty-one planes and damaged nine.

The campaign continued the next day, and again Admiral Yamamoto was out at the field waving as the fliers took off. On April 12, they plastered Port Moresby, flying over the Owen Stanley mountain range with 131 fighters and forty-three medium bombers. In the harbor the Japanese claimed one transport sunk and many fires started, with eleven fires observed and three explosions at Port Moresby. The Allies made light of the bombing, saying it damaged only a few unimportant vessels and a few aircraft on the airstrips, and said nothing about fires and explosions. The Allies put up forty-four fighters. They claimed five Japanese planes shot down, but the Japanese said they had lost seven that day. The Japanese claimed twenty-eight planes destroyed and seven damaged, but the Allies said they had lost no planes in the air and only a handful of the ground. As usual, the claims did not reconcile, because of the over-exuberance of pilots on both sides.

Two days later, April 14, the Japanese struck at Milne Bay. Reconnaissance reports had indicated a grouping of fourteen Allied transports anchored in the harbor and fifty planes on the airfields. The Japanese arrived in two raids: one comprised of seventy-five fighters and twenty-three medium bombers, the other made up of fifty-two fighters and thirty-seven medium bombers. But by the time they arrived, many ships had left the harbor. Still remaining were five corvettes, three transports loaded with troops, a motor ship of 3500 tons at Milne Bay, and several other ships scurrying about to get out to sea.

The Japanese put many hits into the motor ship *Gorgon*,

which became a salvage job, though she did not sink. By the Allied count, the Japanese also sank the transport *Van Heemskerk*, and damaged the *Van Outhoorn*, and strafed a number of vessels. The Allies said the Japanese lost three dive-bombers. But the Japanese claimed entirely different results and losses: five transports sunk, nine transports damaged, several other ships sunk, and fires set at Rabi Airfield. They also said they had lost ten bombers on the two raids but shot down forty-four enemy planes.

The next day, reconnaissance planes over Guadalcanal and New Guinea reported no aerial targets, and so, on April 16, Admiral Yamamoto called off Operation I as a victory. And that it was. He had kept the Allies on the defensive for half a month. But again, it was a pyrrhic victory, because while Yamamoto's fliers were wreaking havoc at Guadalcanal and New Guinea, the wheels were in motion to strengthen the Allied air and naval forces in the war zones. Now that the Germans and Italians were on the run in Tunisia, the Joint Chiefs of Staff were in a better mood to listen to the importunings of Admiral Nimitz's and General MacArthur's people for more ships and planes and guns. Plans had already been made to carry the war to the Japanese, and to seize Rabaul, the major Japanese base for operations in the South and Southwest Pacific. Admiral Halsey was ready to start moving up the Solomons in April, and General MacArthur wanted to clear the Huon Gulf area of New Guinea in May.

The American plans were too ambitious, however. Planes and ships were becoming available, but trained men were still needed to man the weapons, and in the spring of 1943, trained men were still in short supply. Most of the command problems—sorting out fighting men from among the peacetime career officers—had been resolved by 1943. The navy was in the process of selecting thirty more admirals and many more captains to man the ships that were coming off the ways in spring and summer. The unready and the tired had been put out to pasture. Admiral Wilson Brown, who had commanded a carrier task force in the early days of the war, had been "promoted" to be President Roosevelt's naval aide. Rear Admiral Milo F. Draemel, who had served as Nimitz's chief of staff for a little while before it became apparent that his ideas did not fit the modern carrier warfare, had been landed ashore at Philadelphia Naval Yard. Vice Admiral Frank Jack Fletcher, saved from oblivion by Admiral Nimitz's personal loyalty, had ended up as commander of the Northwest Sea Frontier, a shore job where he could not lose any battles, although he offered to take a demotion from vice admiral to rear admiral if he could get back to sea.

New names were appearing on the naval horizon, Admiral Frederick Sherman, Vice Admiral John Hoover, Admiral Daniel Barbey, Rear Admiral R. S. Berkey, Admiral Arthur W. Radford, and many more. These would be the unit commanders and leaders of task forces in the months to come, but they needed seasoning just as much as the marine recruits and the seamen and army infantrymen and fliers did. It would be summer before the American offensive in the Pacific would really swing into action.

CHAPTER EIGHTEEN

New Georgia

April also brought one major change in command in the Pacific War because of an American coup de main.

After Operation I was completed, Admiral Yamamoto decided to make a frontline visit to the major air bases on the Solomons defense chain, to congratulate the men and exhort the fliers and ground personnel to greater heights in the future. The American radio intelligence section of the Pacific Fleet learned of this trip through an intercepted coded message that was decoded and passed along to the leading admirals.

After some debate—because there was only one way the Americans could have discovered Admiral Yamamoto's itinerary—the decision was made to intercept him on his flight and shoot him down. The decision had to be—and was—ratified by President Franklin D. Roosevelt before it could be carried out.

The interception was made by P-38 fighter planes at the tip of Bougainville. Yamamoto's twin-engine bomber and that of his chief of staff were both shot down. The chief of staff survived, but Yamamoto was killed.

The admiral's death created much mourning in Japan, and he was given a state funeral. But what effect it had on the war is a matter for speculation. Perhaps, if the Americans had not been so precipitate, a living Yamamoto might have shortened the war. He was widely known to have opposed its inception and he was the one larger-than-life figure in Japan. Had he still been alive in July 1944, when General Tojo came to the end of his rope and the thinking leaders of Japan realized that the war was lost, Yamamoto might have been the one man who could have brought the war to a less devastating conclusion than the one that came about a year later. As it was, the government floundered to the end.

That is strictly speculative hindsight; what *is* known is that after Yamamoto's death, the appointment of Admiral Mineichi Koga to the position of commander of the Combined Fleet went through swiftly and smoothly, and the war continued as before. At that time, Japan had no more ships, than before, but no fewer. She had a decreasing number of naval aircraft, but Yamamoto himself had not been able to do much about that. There was no indication that the course of the war in the spring of 1943 was at all affected by Yamamoto's death.

Early in May General Imamura appointed Major General Minoru Sasaki commander of the garrison on New Georgia and the Central Solomons. General Sasaki was fresh from Tokyo, where he had served as head of the mechanized department of the army, which meant armor. Immediately he ordered a step-up in the supply missions to Rendova, Kolombangara, and New Georgia. This, then, became the new Japanese defense line in the Solomons.

A step-by-step march along the Solomon Island chain to reach Rabaul on New Britain would take the Americans from Guadalcanal to the Russell Islands, to New Georgia and Vangunu, to Rendova Island, and then across the Slot to Santa Isabel Island, over again to Kolombangara, Vella Lavella, and Choiseul, and thence to the Shortlands (that all-important Japanese naval base) and on to Bougainville. It promised to be a long, hard-slogging campaign, with the Japanese resisting every step of the way, since by the end of June the Allies had occupied only Guadalcanal and the Russells. The next move in Admiral Halsey's plan was to take the Munda air base on New Georgia, thus denying its use to the Japanese as the forward base against Guadalcanal, and giving the Americans a good leg up on the airway to

Rabaul. But that was only part of the plan. Admiral Halsey had ordered the capture of Rendova, the Viru Harbor, Segi Point, and Wickham Anchorage. After that, Admiral Turner was to capture Munda, Kolombangara, and everything else in the New Georgia group, and get ready to march farther up the Solomons chain.

When, in May 1943, the Japanese saw the American buildup beginning at Guadalcanal, they called on Admiral Koga at Truk for naval reinforcement by sea and air for the supply service and for protection from Rabaul. They got them. Ships began bringing supplies and troops to the islands, and General Imamura sent in about a thousand troops. But once again the Japanese army underestimated the problems involved and the number of men needed for the job. Five thousand men would have been more appropriate. The manner of reinforcement was another proof of the continuing arrogance of the Japanese army; the generals could not conceive of being defeated in the war.

On the night of June 20 two American destroyers brought two companies of the Fourth Marine Raider Battalion to Segi Point on the southeastern end of New Georgia Island. Here the seabees were to build another airport. The marines landed safely, and a few hours later two more destroyers brought two companies of the U.S. Army 103rd Infantry Regiment and a naval survey party that would begin preliminary work for the airfield.

On June 27 the marine raiders began a move toward Viru Harbor with the intention of assaulting the small Japanese garrison there. They landed on June 28, and soon got into a fight with the Japanese in which both sides took casualties. This delayed the Americans and threatened to prevent their landing at Viru Harbor in time to take it and prepare the way for the Allied landings scheduled for June 30.

On June 30 the marines attacked the Japanese Viru garrison, which was located at the village of Tetamara. The fighting was fierce, but by 4:30 in the afternoon the marines had taken control, and if there were any Japanese survivors, they had fled into the jungle. Half an hour later the LCT's of the invasion force landed, so it all worked out to what looked like split-second timing.

On June 30 Admiral Turner's amphibious command also launched an invasion on the northern coast of Rendova Island, five miles across Blanche Channel from Munda, having first invested two small islands along the way with troops of the 169th Infantry Regiment. The admiral had expected heavy opposition, but the troops discovered when they landed on Rendova that there were only about 140 fighting sailors and 150 men of the Japanese 229th Infantry Regiment there. In a few hours organized opposition was wiped out.

That same day another small force landed at Wickham Anchorage on New Georgia because Admiral Turner wanted it for a PT boat base. Two destroyers and seven landing craft conducted a very sloppy landing in which six boats were lost by misadventure. Luckily they did not find any Japanese opposition here.

Although the Japanese artillery at Munda could easily reach the American invasion force as it landed on nearby Rendova, the guns did not speak up right away, and the landings were accomplished before the guns fired. Then 4.7-inch shells began raining around the destroyers protecting the transports. One round damaged the destroyer *Gwin* with a shell that struck her in the after engine room and caused ten casualties. The destroyers then laid a smoke screen to cover the invasion forces, and also opened fire on the batteries, which soon shut down their firing. By eight o'clock, all the Japanese batteries at Munda Cape were silent. Rendova was captured, and the Japanese command at Rabaul ordered the soldiers on the island to escape to Munda.

What the Americans were expecting that morning was an attack by a large Japanese force in the air, and they were puzzled because it did not come. The reason it did not, was that, at this same time, over in General MacArthur's Southwest Pacific command, Allied troops were landing at Nassau Bay, seventeen miles from the Japanese base at Salamaua, New Guinea, and in the Trobriand Islands, off the New Guinea shore. At Rabaul, Admiral Kusaka's Eleventh Air Fleet had seventy-one Zero fighters and more than sixty bombers available, but suddenly the admiral was confronted with two new landings on two different fronts, so it was nine o'clock before the first planes took off for Rendova.

Even then Kusaka had to decide how to oppose the New Guinea landings with his bombers, so only a fighter sweep appeared in the Solomons.

The twenty-seven Japanese Zeroes then faced a force of some forty American fighters from Guadalcanal, and the superior American force had the best of it. The struggle, carried on at 21,000 feet, did not affect land operations and was soon over. The Americans claimed to have shot down sixteen Japanese fighters.

All was quiet then at Rendova until mid-afternoon. Then, at 3:30, twenty-six twin-engine bombers escorted by twenty-four fighters appeared, looking for the invasion fleet. It had already turned back toward Guadalcanal, having landed the troops. The Japanese then flew toward Guadalcanal and found the fleet and attacked it. Forty-one American fighters tried to stop the bombers. But the Zeroes did a good job of protecting their bombers and most of them got down to drop their torpedoes. The ships of the invasion fleet opened up with antiaircraft fire, and Admiral Turner, aboard his command ship *McCawley*, counted five bombers shot down. But one bomber put a torpedo into the *McCawley*. The engine room flooded and the ship stopped. Then another bomber came up and dropped its torpedo. The men of the *McCawley* watched it come, straight on, then run alongside the ship from stem to stern, and away.

Admiral Turner moved his flag to the destroyer *Fahrenholt,* and the *McCawley* was taken in tow, first by a transport, and then by a fleet tug. But as the ships moved toward safety that night, two more torpedoes slammed into the *McCawley* and she sank in Blanche Channel.

Next day, Admiral Turner received a glowing report from the Tulagi PT Boat base commander about the exploits of his boys that previous night. They had gone out and found a big "Japanese transport" in Blanche Channel and had sunk her. So the American PT boats had accomplished for the *McCawley* what the Japanese bombers had started the previous afternoon. They had managed to sink the command ship of the American invasion force! Admiral Turner was not pleased. Orders were issued that PT boats would not move in future unless by the admiral's express command.

* * *

On June 30 the Japanese had suffered severe air losses in the South Pacific. Having split their forces and attacked both New Guinea and Solomons operations, they had lost many planes in air battles, and the land-based air forces of Admiral Fitch in the South Pacific and of General Kenney in MacArthur's command had both struck Rabaul air bases with bombers, causing more damage. The night of June 30 Admiral Kusaka called for help from Admiral Koga at Truk. Rabaul had only thirty-five fighters, sixteen bombers, and two scout planes in operating condition, he said. Koga ordered down the Twenty-first Air Group, which meant sixty more fighters, nearly fifty torpedo bombers, and sixteen scout bombers.

The fighting for the New Georgia group did not stop. The American destroyer *Radford* sank the Japanese submarine *R-101*. Japanese fighters and bombers attacked the American positions on the islands and scouted for ships. On July 2, the Japanese army air force took a hand for the first time, in response to the accord worked out by Admiral Kusaka and General Imamura. Twenty-four bombers and thirty army fighters attacked the Rendova beachhead. They came in quietly over the mountains of New Georgia and were undetected until they struck the beachhead, which was alive with troops and supplies. The Americans suffered 150 casualties on the beach and much damage to supply dumps and landing craft.

Nine American fighters were shot down, and the Japanese got away scot free.

That night of July 2, the Japanese "Tokyo Express" operated, as in the days of Guadalcanal. The cruiser *Yubari* and six destroyers came down the Slot with air cover and attacked the Rendova beachhead. But their air intelligence was faulty; they missed the concentrations for the most part and their shells fell in the jungle.

In this first week of July both the Americans and the Japanese made plans for new operations in the Central Solomons. Admiral Halsey ordered the invasion of Munda for July 5. Japanese General Imamura ordered the Munda garrison reinforced on that same day. So the stage was set for a new battle.

Admiral Halsey hurried it up. His intelligence indicated the Japanese had been taken by complete surprise at Rendova and he wanted to take advantage of that factor again before they recovered, so he ordered Major General John H. Hester, commander of the army troops on Rendova, to go by small boat to New Georgia and establish a foothold. The army men found a suitable beach at Zanana, five miles from Munda, and began moving troops over on July 2. At the same time marine Colonel Harry Liversedge was ordered to move his 2600 marines and soldiers to Rice Anchorage, across the strait from Vila, and there to block any attempt by the Japanese to reinforce the Munda area from the nearby Japanese island base of Kolombangara.

The Japanese at Rabaul were planning to retake Rendova, but first they wanted to "soften up" the American forces in the area. For two days they launched extensive air attacks, under the new cooperative plan with the army. After the combined air attack of July 2, which had caused so many casualties on the Rendova beachhead, the Japanese struck again the next day with a fighter sweep, which caught the Americans by surprise and cost them a number of P-38s. But that day the Japanese combined operations did not work very well. The army was supposed to send about half the planes, but the army planes never showed up. Why not? The army said that bad weather had forced their planes from Bougainville to land before they could get to the south.

On July 4 the Japanese hit again, this time with another combined navy-army strike, which attacked the American transport fleet that had just brought more supplies to Rendova. The navy supplied the fighters and the army supplied seventeen bombers. But the Japanese bombers were disorganized, while the American antiaircraft fire was heavy and very accurate. Not so the American reporting of the action. From it, one would have gathered that the Japanese force had been decimated and that only two American landing ships had been damaged when bombs struck between them. The American defenders also claimed to have shot down a dozen bombers and five Zeroes, and that only one Zero escaped their guns.

But the Japanese claims were equally unbelievable. They claimed to have sunk five transports and to have set many dumps on fire. They also claimed to have shot down fourteen Allied fighters, with a loss of only six Japanese bombers, and that each of those bombers had gone to a heroic end, crashing into a ship or a dump and thus justifying the loss.

This Japanese tendency to lionize Japan's fighters was already proving to be one of the weak spots of Japan in the war. No one in authority in Tokyo or in the field seemed to be able to come to grips with the realities; it was too embarrassing for fliers to return to base and admit that many brave men had gone to their deaths without accomplishing anything. This attitude reached from the bottom to the top of the naval and army commands. It was a weakness that had developed only in the days since the battle of Midway. Until that point Japan had been ever victorious, and the exaggerated claims of victories had done no harm. Admiral Yamamoto had recognized, early on, that this exaggeration of success and refusal to admit failure was a fatal flaw, but it was very much a part of the Japanese military character, the character of a nation that had never lost a war.

The American high command, on the contrary, was highly skeptical of claims of success. Admiral King, in particular, tended to disbelieve most reports, and all the commanders took the claims of the aviators with large doses of salt. A classic example of the kind of exaggeration American aviators were prone to is given by Maurice "Pappy" Boyington, who perhaps tells of receiving a letter from his buddies in Squadron 222 while he was in hospital in New Zealand with a broken leg. The letter reported that: "The Japanese had made an all-out air effort when the Marines had gone into New Georgia. During this action the Jap aircraft came so steadily [that] 222 had been ordered to fight until out of fuel and then land in the ocean. . . ."

On July 4 both Japanese and Americans launched their military operations by sea. Colonel Liversedge's troops, including the army contingent, were taken aboard seven destroyer transports headed for New Georgia. That same night Admiral Ainsworth's bombardment force of cruisers and destroyers set off for New Georgia to pave the way for the landings.

And from the other side, came Rear Admiral Teruo Akiyama's reinforcement force of four destroyers, loaded with troops and supplies for Vila, on Kolombangara Island just across a narrow strait from New Georgia. From Vila they would be taken by small craft to Bairoko on New Georgia. Just before midnight, while the Japanese destroyers were unloading, they saw the flashes from the American bombardment group's guns. They abandoned the landing and put to sea. From a long way away the Japanese destroyers fired torpedoes at the vague shapes of the American ships.

Now along came the seven destroyers with the Liversedge detachment aboard. Just after midnight the destroyers transport *Ralph Talbot* picked up two blips on the radar screen, but two minutes later they disappeared at high speed out of range. Ten minutes after that, the destroyer *Strong* of the bombardment force was struck by a torpedo which broke her back. The *Strong* listed to port and stopped suddenly. The destroyers *Chevalier* and *O'Bannon* rushed to the rescue, but the Japanese shore batteries at Bairoko and Enogai began firing, and one of their shells hit the *Strong*. The *O'Bannon* then stopped rescue work and began firing on the shore. The *Strong* was sinking fast, and the men of the *Chevalier* worked quickly to try to save her crew and bring them aboard. They got most of the men, but some were still aboard when the *Strong* went down and her depth charges began to explode. In all, forty-six men of the *Strong* were lost.

The American transport group then stood by while the bombardment group finished its assignment. At one A.M. the bombardment was over, and the transports moved to a point a mile off Rice Anchorage. Men got down into landing craft and rubber rafts to go ashore. The Japanese shore batteries then shifted their fire to the landing parties, and the American destroyers fired at them. There were no hits on the landing craft. The landing was completed by six A.M., and the destroyers retired toward Guadalcanal. The drive to capture Munda airfield had begun.

The next step in the struggle came on July 5, when Admiral Akiyama again came back south with the destroyers to reinforce Kolombangara and New Georgia. He came with an augmented force of three groups of destroyers which left the advance base at Buin, headed for Vila again. From aerial observation and coast watchers Admiral Halsey was being kept well informed, and this day he learned that a large number of Japanese destroyers were on the move, so he ordered Admiral Ainsworth and the bombardment force, who were in Indispensable Strait off the southern coast of Guadalcanal, to stop their plans for refuelling in a quiet zone and hasten back to New Georgia to do battle. Ainsworth had three cruisers, the *Helena*, the *Honolulu*, and the *St. Louis*, and four destroyers.

As they moved toward battle in Kula Gulf, both the Japanese and the Americans were confident. The Americans felt secure because their cruisers had six-inch guns to the Japanese cruisers' five-inch, and because they had begun to be familiar with their radar and it made a lot of difference in their night-fighting ability. The Japanese were proud of their own night-fighting ability, and contemptuous of the Americans', based on the activities in the Slot in the past year. Also, the Japanese themselves were now getting radar; Admiral Akiyama's flagship, the destroyer *Niizuki*, had a radar set.

As day dawned on day July 6, Admiral Akiyama sent three destroyers to move close along the coast of Kolombangara and head for Vila to begin the unloading of supplies and men. Meanwhile, he took his other seven destroyers down the center of Kula Gulf, looking for a fight.

The move was plotted on the American radar screens, and at that point the radar showed the Japanese to be sixteen miles away. Admiral Ainsworth assumed battle position: two destroyers out in front, three cruisers in a line, and two destroyers bringing up the rear. Ainsworth noticed that several ships had split off from the main group, but the mountains of Kolombangara disturbed the radar plotting so that his intelligence was a little vague as to detail.

The Americans had no sooner assumed this new formation than Admiral Akiyama knew all about it from his ship's radar system. He ordered the Japanese destroyers to up their speed to 30 knots and get ready to launch torpedoes.

Just before two A.M. the American cruisers began firing by radar on the Japanese. Their shells hit home on the *Niizuki*, and the flagship was soon sinking. But the other two destroyers with her, the *Suzukaze* and the *Tanikaze*, launched torpedoes as ordered, and sixteen "fish" headed toward the American formation. The American cruisers continued to fire, using radar-directed gunnery, with vastly improved accuracy as compared to earlier battles. They hit the *Suzukaze*, knocking out the ship's searchlight and starting fires. They hit the *Tanikaze*, too, but the shells were duds and did very little damage.

Having fired their torpedoes and taken gunfire, the two Japanese destroyers in the van turned about, made smoke, and ran out of the battle area to reload their torpedo tubes.

The American destroyer captains wanted to use torpedoes, but Admiral Ainsworth insisted that they wait and fire their guns instead. So they began firing at the other Japanese destroyers. Admiral Ainsworth then "crossed the T," a maneuver in which he moved across the top of the enemy column of ships. That meant that his ships could all fire on the enemy line, but the enemy ships, except for their leader, were constrained by the angle. This was how battles had been won since the days of sail. Yet for some reason, the formula did not work for Admiral Ainsworth this night. The first Japanese ship in the line, the *Amagiri*, was unhurt. The second, the *Hatsuyuki*, was hit by three shells, but they were all duds. Then the Japanese destroyer captains broke the line, and the advantage was gone as they headed for Vila.

Admiral Ainsworth called on the cruiser *Helena* and the others to start after the enemy ships headed for Vila, but he got no answer from the *Helena*. The reason: she was sunk, hit by three of those sixteen torpedoes fired at the outset of the battle. Her bow had been blown off first torpedo, her back was broken by the second, and the third finished the job. She folded up and sank swiftly, in 1800 feet of water.

Admiral Ainsworth might have headed for Vila with his cruisers and continued the battle there. But he had the mistaken impression that he had sunk several ships and that the others were scurrying back towards Rabaul in disarray, so he did not go to Vila. He sent the destroyers *Nicholas* and *Radford* to rescue survivors as soon as he learned that the *Helena* had sunk, and then headed back for Tulagi, much concerned about his fuel and ammunition supplies. His cruisers had fired all but about ten rounds for each gun.

The troop-carrying Japanese destroyers reached Vila and unloaded their men and supplies. One, the *Nagatsuki* went awry when her captain took a shortcut across unfamiliar water and ran the ship aground on reef. She stuck fast. Another Japanese destroyer tried to pull her off, but it was impossible.

Amagiri, picking up survivors from the sunken *Niizuki*, ran afoul of the American destroyers *Nicholas* and *Radford*, which were rescuing the survivors of the *Helena*. All ships fired torpedoes at each other, but no one hit anything, thus. The Americans scored some shell hits on the *Amigiri*. This frightened *Amigiri*'s the captain so much that he delayed the rescue operations and left three hundred men struggling in the water, including Admiral Akiyama, who was lost that night. The *Amagiri* went off smoking, toward Rabaul.

The two American destroyers then found the Japanese destroyer *Mochizuki* by radar and stopped their rescue attempts to do battle again. They started firing, and the *Mochizuki* began to smoke. The Americans thought they had given her a mortal wound and reported as much. Then came the dawn and with it the fear of a new Japanese air attack, since enemy air action had been so great in previous days. So the two American destroyers also suspended rescue operations, leaving four boats in the water, and headed for friendly shores.

Morning having come, so did the aircraft of both sides. The Americans vastly outnumbered the Japanese in the sky this morning, and they attacked the grounded *Nagatsuki*, but the Zeroes fought them off. Finally both sides ran out of gas, and flew off. In the afternoon a flight of B-25 bombers appeared, coming in low and using the new skip-bombing techniques invented by General Kenney's Fifth Air Force, and set the Japanese destroyer afire. That night the magazines exploded and that was the end of the *Nagatsuki*. Her crew had fought all day on the stranded vessel, but got off and made their way to Kolombangara, where they disappeared into the jungle.

So the Battle of Kula Gulf ended. The Americans thought they had scored a signal victory, mistaking the concealment smoke made by several destroyers as smoke from fires. The

Japanese claimed nothing for a change. They had lost an admiral and two destroyers, but they had sunk an American cruiser and more important as far as the Japanese navy was concerned, they had carried out their supply mission.

CHAPTER NINETEEN

Munda

Looking at the action in the Solomons as of the summer of 1943, one has to conclude that the Japanese army really had not learned much about its enemies in the long months of the Guadalcanal campaign. Imperial General Headquarters still seemed to be operating on the assumption that a Japanese army unit was capable of defeating an enemy ten times as strong. At first, perhaps, they could have been forgiven this arrogance because, as the record showed they had done very well in Malaya, the Dutch East Indies, and less well, but well enough, in the Philippines. But there was no man in the army who seemed to have the understanding of the Americans that Admiral Yamamoto had, and for the first year of the Solomons campaign the mistakes made by the Japanese generals were enormous and repetitive.

Rendova, for example, was garrisoned at the time of the Allied invasion by just over three hundred men. For weeks before the Allied invasion that they had seen coming, the troops on Rendova had wondered why they were not reinforced. Their concerns shows in the soldiers diaries captured by the invading forces. But General Imamura and his staff admitted to being completely surprised by the Rendova landings. They simply had not believed that the Americans could stage a major invasion just a few months after the Gua-

147

dalcanal withdrawal. Again, they had underestimated the strength of their enemy.

As General Sasaki, on New Georgia, contemplated his problems of defense at the beginning of July 1943, he called for reinforcements. He had been allotted only a single regiment to defend New Georgia and he knew it was not enough. But Rabaul's answer had been to dispatch a measly 1000 men, about a battalion, which was nowhere near enough to defend the island.

General Sasaki had concentrated his defenses around the Munda airfield, which was natural enough, but that left the rest of the island pretty much open to the invaders. Colonel Liversedge's force heading for Bairoko created the greatest threat, because Bairoko had the best port on New Georgia. On July 5, Liversedge's men were on the banks of the Giza Giza River. That day they moved out toward Bairoko. A battalion of the 148th Army Infantry was diverted to the Munda-Bairoko trail to set up a roadblock.

Colonel Liversedge then took the remainder of his Northern Force toward Enogai Inlet, where he expected a major engagement with the Japanese. Meanwhile, eight miles away as the crow flies, but through almost impenetrable jungle, General Hester was not making much progress in his drive toward Munda, and he faced Japanese troops dug in on the Sho River, not far from his landing point of Zanana.

The Japanese of the single battalion of the 229th Infantry, who had been given the job of stopping General Hester, numbered only about 1000 men. But what they lacked in numbers, they made up in fierceness and skill. The Japanese quickly estimated that the Americans numbered 11,000 men, and they expected a swift attack against their positions. When it did not come, they decided they could handle the situation and they began a fright campaign against the Americans.

General Hester put the 172nd Regimental Combat Team on the left and the 169th on the right of his force. Their objective was the Bairoko River, but they moved very slowly, unused to the climate and the terrain.

The Japanese began their fright campaign as night fell. They crawled through the jungle infiltrating the American lines, making animal noises, giving birdcalls when there were no birds about, attacking foxholes and stabbing the inmates by the light of flares that illuminated their targets and added to the sinister pyschological effect. By July 8 they had succeeded in unnerving the American soldiers, who had had virtually no sleep for three nights. The result was indiscriminate American firing at night, which wounded many other Americans. A further result was that in four days the army force had moved only a mile and a half along the trail to Munda.

The Japanese facing the Liversedge marine force had nowhere near that success because the marines had been trained to face just such activity. At night they held their positions, stayed in their foxholes, and repelled any attempted invasion of their territory. Doggedly, the Liversedge force moved ahead, though not as fast as the colonel wanted. On July 7 they reached Maranusa, and in a trail fight that day they secured from the Japanese maps of the Enogai and Bairoko defenses.

General Sasaki was ready for a fight and hoped for reinforcement, but from Rabaul came nothing but silence. For the moment Sasaki was confident because the army troops of the Hester command were so inept, but he fully expected another landing and a major Allied effort against Munda soon. He asked for orders from Rabaul as well as reinforcements. The answer again was silence. On July 8 he warned Rabaul that if they did nothing the Japanese forces would be overrun by superior strength. He proposed a counterattack to destroy the Liversedge force, and finally both the Eighth Fleet and Eighth Army agreed. So on the evening of July 8 the Japanese began sending troops from Kolombangara to Bairoko by barge.

On July 9, the marines began marching on Enogai. They were marching on empty stomachs because they had run out of supplies. They reached the area, but they did not capture Enogai that day, and went to sleep that night hungry again.

Meanwhile, the Japanese Third Battalion of the Thirteenth Infantry Regiment had reached Bairoko by barge. They set out along the Bairoko-Munda trail, where the army troops of Colonel Liversedge had set up the road block. The

Japanese were heading down to make an attack on General Hester's army force.

On the morning of July 10, Colonel Liversedge's men received a welcome airdrop of food that revived them enough to surge down on the Enogai garrison and capture the warehouse there. They found it full of rice. Bliss! At dark they set up defense perimeter at Enogai Point.

Meanwhile, on July 10 the Japanese on the Bairoko-Munda trail ran into the roadblock. They fought, suffering a hundred casualties, but broke through the American line and met Japanese guides who took them down the trail toward Munda, where they arrived on July 12. They had left detachments behind to engage the Liversedge column, and soon it was reported that these detachments were being overwhelmed by the marines. General Sasaki had no reserves to send to reinforce the Bairoko trail.

On the night of July 11, Enogai was reinforced (for the Americans) by troops and supplies from Rice Anchorage. Then Colonel Liversedge turned his attention to the move against Munda.

In the Zanana area General Hester was making no progress. A naval bombardment mission from Guadalcanal did not help, because Hester called for shooting so far from his own lines that the Japanese simply moved up and escaped the shelling. For forty minutes, four cruisers and ten destroyers cut up a lot of New Georgia jungle, but that was about all they accomplished. On July 12, the Japanese cut the trail between the 172nd Infantry and the 169th and left the former unit in deep jungle without supplies. The troops were only a quarter of a mile from their objective, Laiana Beach, but the terrain was all muddy swamp.

That day Colonel Liversedge waited at the roadblock, but the Japanese were now using two other trails from Bairoko to Munda, so there was no action. General Hester was stuck in the mud. The next step was to take Munda, but that depended on the Hester troops. Everybody waited.

On July 13 the Japanese were reinforced at Munda, and General Sasaki made ready to counterattack. He had received some good news: Rabaul had become upset to learn that the Americans had seized Enogai, and had decided to take strong action. Admiral Kusaka had sent Rear Admiral

Shunji Izaki with a cruiser and four destroyers to escort four destroyer transports bearing 1300 more troops of the Thirteenth Regiment to reinforce General Sasaki.

When Allied coast watchers saw the Japanese ships moving down toward the Slot, they informed Noumea, and Admiral Halsey sent Admiral Ainsworth with an augmented cruiser force to intercept the enemy. Ainsworth had the cruisers *Honolulu* and *St. Louis*, the New Zealand cruiser *Leander*, and ten destroyers under his command.

These days the Americans seemed constantly to be getting new equipment. They now had Black Cats, radar-equipped PBY bombers, that flew at night and could find the enemy by their radar. A Black Cat gave the word to Admiral Ainsworth about the coming of the Japanese from the north. At midnight they were twenty-five miles from the American cruiser force. Admiral Ainsworth moved confidently to attack, intending to destroy the Japanese with gunfire before they knew he was there. What a difference radar made!

Or did it? Admiral Izaki already knew where the Americans were, for although he did not have radar, he did have electronic equipment that could detect radar. He had known the position of the oncoming Americans for two hours.

At one A.M. on July 13, Admiral Ainsworth's radar screen showed one big blip and five little blips. The admiral turned his column to the right to attack, and ordered his destroyers to start firing torpedoes. Admiral Izaki gave the same order to his destroyers.

Admiral Ainsworth held course for a few minutes and then unleashed the six-inch guns of the cruisers. All three cruisers were firing at the big blip, the Japanese cruiser *Jintsu*. In ten minutes they had fired 2600 shells at her. Perhaps twenty struck home—not very many, but they did the job. The *Jintsu* broke in two and the two halves drifted apart, burning, before they sank. Admiral Izaki was lost, and with him, 480 Japanese seamen.

But before the *Jintsu* went down she hit the *Leander* with a salvo, damaging her radio antennae. Then came the "long lance" torpedoes, for which Admiral Ainsworth again was not ready. Belatedly, he ordered a turn to the south, but that meant that the *Leander* turned right into a torpedo, which put her out of the fight. The destroyers *Jenkins* and

Radford stood by the *Leander*. The Japanese destroyers moved away to reload torpedoes, and above the battle the pilot of the Black Cat reported that the Japanese had been routed and were retreating at high speed. Admiral Ainsworth believed this story, partly because his cruiser and destroyer captains were all reporting and their reports added up to the destruction of six ships. So, it seemed, the battle was over.

He sent three destroyers (or so he thought) to chase the retreating Japanese back to the Shortlands if necessary and sink the damaged ships. But the destroyer captains did not get the message right. They understood that Ainsworth was withdrawing, and so they headed back down the Slot.

The Japanese had ducked into a squall and in fifteen minutes they reloaded their torpedo tubes, then turned back to fight. Meanwhile the four troop-carrying destroyers were discharging their 1300 reinforcements on the coast of Kolombangara.

When Admiral Ainsworth heard nothing from the three destroyers, the *Nicholas*, the *O'Bannon*, and the *Taylor*, which he had sent after the "retreating" Japanese, he turned north and tried to find the enemy. Just before two A.M. the radar man of the cruiser *Honolulu* reported five blips on the radar screen; they were twelve miles off. Admiral Ainsworth called his destroyers. He had been observing radio silence and was out of contact.

Captain Yoshima Shimai, the destroyer division commander, had taken over command of the Japanese forces when he saw that the *Jintsu* was sinking, and he was coming south at high speed now to attack. At two A.M. Shimai saw the American ships and gave the order to attack. Because, during the first part of the action, Shimai had seen the Americans turn to the right to begin firing, he figured that they would do it again, and sent the torpedoes off to the right to intercept them. The ships fired their torpedoes, swung around and raced away again. Sure enough, Admiral Ainsworth having watched the ships on the radar screen, completed his roll call, and decided the screen ships were enemy, turned sharp to the right to begin firing.

The American ships turned directly into the line of approach of the Japanese torpedoes.

A lookout on the *Honolulu* saw them first, and shouted

as the initial torpedo passed. The next hit the *Honolulu* in the bow, and the third smashed onto the *St. Louis*. Another torpedo plowed into the destroyer *Gwin*, which promptly blew up.

Admiral Ainsworth had already radioed in the word of his incredible, wonderful victory. As a result, when he limped into Tulagi carrying the survivors of one destroyer, with three damaged cruisers—one so badly crippled that it was out of the war for good—he was greeted by a brass band and his men were told that they were heroes.

It was not true, of course, and Admirals Halsey and Nimitz soon set that matter to rights, but in a way, it *was* a victory for the Americans, a victory for American power. For by this point in the war, the Americans could afford to lose a destroyer and have three cruisers damaged, while the Japanese could ill-afford to lose a single light cruiser. Attrition had begun to wear the Japanese down, and even the fact that the transport destroyers had completely succeeded in their mission could not efface the disappointment of losing another admiral and another big fighting ship.

General Sasaki was very pleased with the news that he had another 1300 men to fight with, but the fact remained that he was still being shorted by the high command at Rabaul. A staff officer had suggested that General Imamura send the entire Sixth Division to defend Munda, but the suggestion was ignored. What the Japanese could not seem to get through their heads was the enormous power that the Americans would be able to bring against them. Just at this point Admiral Turner was asking Admiral Halsey for 25,000 troops to throw into the New Georgia battle.

Between July 13 and 16, Colonel Liversedge was bogged down, waiting for General Hester to move. General Sasaki ordered the newly arrived Thirteenth Infantrymen to attack the flank of General Hester's 169th Infantry. He also asked Rabaul by radio for more reinforcements. Rabaul did not reply, but the advance elements of the Thirteenth Infantry moved out, and soon had the 169th Infantry cut off deep in the jungle.

General Hester asked for more troops and Major General Oscar Griswold, commander of the XIV Corps on Guadalcanal, relayed the message to Admiral Halsey. Halsey wondered what was going on and sent Lieutenant General Millard Harmon up front to find out. When Harmon arrived at New Georgia and visited Hester's command post he was appalled at the confusion and incompetence he found. He relieved General Hester of command, but there was nobody in the whole area to replace him, so Harmon told General Griswold that he would have to step down from his corps command temporarily and take over the troops in the field.

General Griswold had hardly time to get set when he was attacked by Colonel Tomonari's Thirteenth Infantry in the Zanana area. The Japanese tanks, machine guns and many 155-mm field guns. But now the Cactus Air Force from Guadalcanal took a hand, and in spite of strong air support for the Japanese from Rabaul, the Americans kept the Japanese from wiping out the American force.

Actually, General Hester had been right. He did need more troops than he had been given, largely because the American army troops were so poorly trained. And Griswold brought the troops in, the Forty-third U.S. Army Division. But even these reinforcements did not bring Allied victory. Colonel Tomonari attacked and attacked, and each time he won a limited victory. The poor 169th Infantry combat team was cut off in the jungle for two weeks, supplied only by air. Finally, it was rescued.

The factor that permitted survival of the bridgehead during this vital period turned out not even to be the air forces, which gave heroic support, but the American artillery operating from Oniavisi Island across the lagoon from the Zanana Beach. It kept the Japanese from scoring a final victory.

General Griswold brought in a half dozen marine tanks, but one by one they were knocked out. New Georgia was not good tank country and the Japanese blew them up.

On July 18, Colonel Liversedge finally got the reinforcement he had requested, the Fourth Marine Raider Battalion from Segi Point, which came in by destroyer transport. Liversedge then planned an attack on Bairoko for July 20. He made the attack, but it was disastrous. The Japanese defenses were four tiers deep and he could only penetrate the first two tiers. The marines fought all day long at Bairoko, suffering more than 250 casualties, and retreated back to Enogai. That night the Japanese reinforced Bairoko again by barge.

At this point in the defense of New Georgia, General Sasaki was winning, but his pleas for support were going unanswered at Rabaul, while General Griswold was bringing in all the resources his XIV Corps could provide, and the American navy and Cactus Air Force were running every mission they could. In the battle for New Georgia, American air power was making the difference. On July 19, for example, the Japanese sent a reinforced troop-carrying force to New Georgia under the command of Rear Admiral Shoji Nishimura. The force comprised three cruisers, one light cruiser, and nine destroyers. Bombers from Henderson Field sank the destroyer *Yugure* and damaged the cruiser *Kumano*. The destroyer *Kiyonami*, standing by to rescue survivors of the *Yugure*, was caught by B-25s. The B-25s then unleashed the kind of skip-bombing attack that had been so successful in the Bismarck Sea, and sank the *Kiyonami*.

Three days later the Japanese sent another mission to the Shortlands, including three destroyers laden with troops and supplies and the seaplane carrier *Nisshin*, which was carrying an artillery battalion and its guns and equipment. American bombers caught the convoy in Bougainville Strait and sank the *Nisshin* and all the artillery.

Meanwhile the battered force of Colonel Liversedge was resupplied by four destroyer transports. They were protected by a convoy of two cruisers and five destroyers which came into Enogai Roads.

On land the battle went on, and on. The Americans concentrated on artillery, air, and naval bombardment. The Japanese staged many ground attacks and usually gained ground, but could not bring about a decisive action. General Sasaki just did not have the resources, though nobody at Rabaul seemed to realize this fact.

The Americans were gearing up for a major onslaught, because Halsey insisted on it. His insistence was based in part on his shortage of certain materials, particularly landing craft, which he had to share with General MacArthur's operations in the Southwest Pacific theater.

Japanese and Americans both planned offensives for July

25. General Sasaki's offensive never got off the ground, but General Griswold's did, starting with a destroyer bombardment off the Munda airfield area, and followed by a bombing raid and an artillery barrage. Then came tanks and shock troops with flame throwers, bazookas, 75-mm pack howitzers, and lesser equipment to hit the Japanese pillboxes of the defensive positions. By the end of the day the Americans had destroyed seventy-five pillboxes. But that night, the Japanese infiltrated through the lines and reoccupied many of them. So the job had to be done all over again the next day. The Japanese defenses were built around hilly positions and they contested every foot of ground. Marines and soldiers fought for every inch, and General Sasaki's defenses crumbled, slowly but certainly. He still got no word from Rabaul. The battle raged on. By August 1, the Japanese were down to 1200 defenders at Munda, but still they fought savagely.

And what was Rabaul doing?

It was paying much more attention to reinforcing the Shortlands and Bougainville then to saving Munda. It was as if Rabaul had already written off New Georgia, which really was the case. General Imamura was beginning to see the handwriting on the wall, with American victories in New Guinea and in the Solomons, and the growing power of the United States at sea and in the air. His strategy now was based on delay, with the pious hope that somehow Tokyo would produce the resources to bring him out of his predicament. But every day the Americans advanced, and on August 2, the Forty-third Division troops reached the edge of the Munda airfield. Two days later the troops of the Thirty-seven Division broke through the Japanese line six-hundred yards north of the airfield. On August 5, the fight was over. General Sasaki evacuated his survivors to Kolombangara Island.

More than at Guadalcanal, the American victory at New Georgia was one of preponderant force, with two infantry divisions and the marines involved on the ground, and very important air support and naval support. Two thousand Japanese soldiers were killed in the battle for Munda: the Allies suffered 1150 casualties. With their superior commitment of manpower, they could afford to press the battle.

In the end, General Sasaki and a sad remnant of 1300 survivors left for Kolombangara. Many hundreds of Japanese holed up on New Georgia were routed out in time. One Japanese source estimated that the Japanese had lost 12,000 troops in the defense of the New Georgia group, a figure that seems extremely high, even if it includes the naval and air losses. But one thing was certain, the New Georgia struggle, unlike Guadalcanal, was one in which the Allies had the upper hand all the way. Japanese power was not proving adequate for the tasks imposed on it, and American power was increasing every day.

CHAPTER TWENTY

Change in Strategy

General Sasaki did not know it as he struggled so manfully to defend Munda airfield and Japan's hold on New Georgia, but he and his men in the Central Solomons were sacrificial lambs on the altar of the army's revision of basic strategy.

The cornerstone of General Tojo's policy as prime minister was the solution to the "China Incident." Most of Japan's troops were tied up in China, Manchuria, or along the Korean border with USSR. There was still an element inside the Japanese establishment that looked to a "strike north" and once General Tojo himself had been a leading advocate of war with Russia. But now Tojo was beleagured by the obviously growing power of the Americans and the diminishing resources of Japan.

In China, the Japanese army continued to be bogged down, holding the cities along the eastern seaboard, but unable to capture the west, and harried wherever garrisons were small. The activity in China continued to be holding action, and the occasional "new campaigns" always ended by bogging down.

Tojo's naval advisors in the summer of 1943 warned of a coming campaign across the Central Pacific. It was well known that the American navy war plan called for such a drive. It was also known that General MacArthur wanted to carry the war from New Guinea up to the Philippines. Tojo was very skeptical about the Central Pacific drive be-

158

cause he had no real understanding of America and very little respect for that country. But he also saw how great was the expenditure of resources to hold the South and Southwest Pacific, where it was now apparent that Japan's reach had exceeded her grasp. The fact was that the original Japanese war plan had never conceived of a push so far as Rabaul or a threat to Port Moresby and Australia. All this had come about in the euphoria that overcame the Japanese military establishment with the ease of the first victories. By the summer of 1943 it was apparent that the dream of taking Australia would have to be abandoned.

Faced with the realities, Tojo had stood for the evacuation of Guadalcanal in the discussions at the end of 1942. He had acted as prime minister and as war minister, a post he had also assumed. He had been opposed by General Shinichi Tanaka, chief of operations of the Imperial General Headquarters, and by Colonel Takushiro Hattori, the plans officer. The argument had been long and bitter. In the end Tanaka and Hattori were both transferred out of Imperial General Headquarters to garrison posts (sent to Siberia) and Tojo brought in flunkeys to replace them. That was the end of army unity; from that point until the fall of Saipan, Tojo would have his own way just now that way not only meant further retrenchment, but also switching form an offensive policy to a defensive policy.

With a new military campaign in central China, Tojo still hoped to bring about a coup that would resolve the problem of China, and he remained confident that if he could solve *that* problem, he could make an accomodation with the Western powers. All this was a result of his real belief that the Westerners were too weak to stand up to Japan in the final analysis. Until that accomodation could be made, he said, Japan would tighten her belt and wait. "Ichioku ichigan" (100 million people as one bullet) was the current slogan in Japan.

The decision had been made months earlier, but even Rabaul had not been told. Everything and everyone south of the "Inner Empire" was going to be expendable. For the moment the line had been drawn from Truk-Rabaul to Biak-Java. But in Tojo's mind only this was only a temporary arrangement. He was not concerned with the navy's arguments for bases. He was interested only in the empire and the Asian mainland—and the Dutch East Indies, because he had to be (there was no gainsaying the need for oil).

That summer of 1943 Prime Minister Tojo did two things of note outside his normal sphere of activity. First, he put into motion the long-discussed plan for a cooperative sphere called the Greater East Asia Empire. Burma was to become "independent" and allied to Japan, as Thailand already was. Wang Ching Wei's puppet government of China was a part of the empire. So was Emperor Pu Yi's Manchukuo, and so was José Laurel's Philippines. In the Indies, the Japanese gave much authority to the Indonesians. But it was all done to make use of the resources of these areas to the fullest for the Japanese war effort.

Prime Minister Tojo's second noteworthy action that summer was to make a swing around the empire; he went to Rabaul to see for himself what was happening. He returned convinced that Rabaul and everything south of it had to be regarded as expendable. Already so many planes, so many pilots, so much war material had been expended in the South Pacific that it had affected the whole war effort. In the future, everything was to be scaled down. Destroyers, in particular, were not to be put at special risk. The Japanese had lost forty destroyers in the past fourteen months, and Japanese shipyards did not have the capacity to replace them. Thus Japanese retrenchment affected the fleet for the first time.

The Combined Fleet began to retract and restrict their activity, just when the Americans began to expand theirs. In the battle for Munda the American destroyers began to perform superbly for the first time. The destroyer captains had long claimed they had been restricted by fleet practices that kept them from operating aggressively. But the facts of previous naval battles indicate that throughout the Guadalcanal campaign, American destroyer operations were far inferior to those of the enemy. During the New Georgia campaign, however, all this changed. There were several reasons for this. One of the most important was that American radar and the use of it were vastly improved.

* * *

On July 23 Commander Arleigh Burke took a supply convoy up to Enogai. In an hour and a half his ships landed their supplies and took off the men wounded in action against the Japanese. They were bombarded by the Japanese shore guns as they stood out to sea on the morning of the 24th, but escaped unscathed. They then returned to their anchorage at Purvis Bay on Florida Island—but not to rest. That same night they set out on a bombardment mission and at six A.M. on July 25 Commander Burke's six destroyers bombarded the Lambeti Plantation, which lay between Munda airfield and Laiana.

They fired four thousand rounds of five-inch ammunition in a raid very much like the Japanese raids on Henderson Field. But, as the experts later discovered, the Japanese escaped its worst effects by moving out of the area, close to the American lines, and moving back to their pillboxes when the bombardment was over.

The pillboxes were stoutly constructed, so much so that Admiral Wilkinson later said that they would withstand everything but a direct hit, and that it would have taken three times the number of shells fired to make any real impression on the land battlefield. After the war, when the Strategic Bombing Survey was conducted, much doubt was cast on air force claims to damage. The same could be said, as marine commanders sometimes observed, of the naval bombardments conducted during the war. This one, in particular, was very destructive to the old coco palm plantation, but not to the Japanese. It took artillery fire, men and tanks, to get at those pillboxes, and even then, they literally had to be ripped apart to keep the Japanese from reoccupying them. But that was not the fault of the destroyer men.

Chance gave the destroyer men the opportunity to prove their worth at the end of the first week of August. At the time Admiral Wilkinson learned that the Japanese were scheduled to run a section of the Tokyo Express to Kolombangara on the following night. Admiral Wilkinson was the new amphibious commander in the South Pacific, for Admiral Turner had just been ordered back to Pearl Harbor to begin planning the invasion of the Gilberts, scheduled for the autumn of 1943.

Admiral T. S. Wilkinson wanted to stop the Japanese

effort, but his cruisers were far away. There were the destroyers at the base near Tulagi, however, and Admiral Wilkinson, who was an old destroyer man himself, decided to give them a responsibility they had not enjoyed before.

The senior officer present was Commander Frederick Moosbrugger, who had just come in as commander of Destroyer Division 12. He was ordered to take his three operating destroyers, the *Dunlap*, *Craven*, and *Maury* and Destroyer Division 15's *Lang*, *Sterett*, and *Stack*, on a sweep of Vella Gulf.

Moosbrugger conferred with Admiral Wilkinson and was advised to stand off and use radar gunnery because he could expect the Japanese to be the more skillful with their torpedoes, which were better than the Americans'. This was the conventional wisdom of the day in the South Pacific.

But in Commander Moosbrugger and Destroyer Division 12, the South Pacific had something new: a destroyer division that was confident of its own ability with torpedoes and not afraid to face the enemy. Moosbrugger had served in this division since before Pearl Harbor and had trained in night torpedo attacks. At last skilled American destroyer men were coming into the South Pacific action. And on this occasion Admiral Wilkinson gave the destroyer men their head. "You know your ships better than I do," he told Commander Moosbrugger, "It's up to you how to fight them."

Moosbrugger's destroyer force was a mixed bag. Because the Japanese had, at the end of the Guadalcanal campaign, lost so many destroyers on the supply run, they had recently been using barges called *daihatsu*, armored on the sides, to carry perhaps one-hundred troops or fifteen tons of cargo, with guns as large as 37-mm. Some American destroyers had sacrificed half their torpedo capacity to mount 40-mm guns for attacks on the barges. The three destroyers of Division 15 were so armed, with four five-inch guns like any destroyers, but with four 20-mm guns and four 40-mm guns as well, which meant they could only carry eight torpedoes instead of the usual sixteen. Moosbrugger's division was standard, with eight 20-mm guns and sixteen torpedoes. Therefore Commander Moosbrugger planned that if the "Tokyo Express" consisted of destroyers, his division would attack first; if it consisted of the fifty-foot-long *daihatsu*, Commander Rodger W. Simpson's Division 15 would attack first.

Before the destroyers set out, Commander Moosbrugger instructed the torpedo men to disconnect the magnetic exploders, because he did not trust them. These were the same exploders that had caused the submariners so much trouble in the past two years.

The destroyers left Tulagi at 11:30 on the morning of August 6, and steamed south of Savo Island and New Georgia, aiming for Gizo Strait, which separates Kolombangara Island from tiny Gizo Island. At noon they had word from search planes about a "fast fleet" spotted north of Buka, and they estimated the enemy ships would reach Vella Gulf by midnight. Darkness came, and with it rainsqualls, as they approached Gizo Strait. Commander Simpson's division stayed close to shore, looking for *daihatsu*. Commander Moosbrugger led his division down the middle, approaching Blackett Strait.

At this same time, Captain Kaju Sugiura in the *Hagikaze* was leading the *Arashi*, the *Kawakaze*, and the *Shigure*, laden with troops and supplies toward Kolombangara. At noon, when spotted by the American search plane, he knew he had been seen, but kept right on. He had run this same mission four nights earlier quite successfully. This night he planned to enter Vella Gulf at 11:30, and appeared right on schedule. Ten minutes later the Americans had the Japanese ships on their radar, four vessels heading toward them at over 25 knots.

Commander Moosbrugger's radar gave the data to the torpedo directors. The Americans were tracking the enemy, and still the Japanese had not seen them. At 11:41 the *Dunlap*, the *Craven*, and the *Maury* each fired eight torpedoes at the enemy, at that time four miles away. Then Moosbrugger ordered a turn, and each ship heeled over in a right-angled turn—to escape any torpedoes that might have been fired by the Japanese.

The Japanese were completely unaware of the approach of the enemy. They were expecting anything but a destroyer attack. PT boats, yes. Night bombers, yes. But destroyers?

The Japanese had little but contempt for the operation of American destroyers in this war.

Aboard the *Hagikaze*, lookouts saw all sorts of things in the night, PT boats (where there were none) and misty black forms. Another destroyer reported a wake on the port bow. Still another reported one on the starboard bow. Then, at 11:43, a lookout aboard the flagship reported four destroyers swinging rapidly to starboard, and her torpedo men set to work. But the Japanese were not expecting trouble this night and the torpedo men were not alert. The torpedo director operator was actually taking a nap and the torpedo men were serving as lookouts. And then the American torpedoes came in. The *Hagikaze* was hit first by two torpedoes. The *Arashi* got it next, with three "fish." The *Kawakaze* was then hit by a torpedo that blew up her magazine and sent half the ship flashing into the sky. The *Shigure* alone was unhurt; the torpedoes around her ran deep (another American problem) and passed harmlessly beneath her hull. The *Shigure* fired eight torpedoes, made smoke, and retired to reload. Her torpedoes did not hit any American ships.

By the light from the fires that developed aboard the stricken Japanese ships the American destroyers opened up with five-inch guns. The *Kawakaze* sank. The gunners of the *Arashi* and the *Hagikaze* fired wildly in all directions, but soon stopped firing. Just after midnight the *Arashi*'s magazine exploded, whereupon the *Shigure*, which was heading back into the battle, reversed course and got out of the area. The *Hagikaze*, now the object of fire from all six American destroyers, exploded eight minutes after the *Arashi*.

The American destroyers then moved through the Japanese wreckage, seeing heads bobbing in the water and trying to rescue Japanese sailors, but finding no takers. So the destroyers went home, all unscathed. The one casualty of the night was a gun loader whose hand was crushed in an accident.

As for the Japanese, it was a night of total failure. The *Shigure* made it back to base, but the mission was a disaster. Fifteen hundred sailors and soldiers had been lost, and all that supply. Three hundred Japanese made it to Vella Lavella Island. They arrived wet and bedraggled, just a week before the Americans launched an invasion of this almost-deserted island.

The American invasion of Vella Lavella came on August 15, led by four American PT boats that had landed scouts hours before to mark the beaches at Barakoma, a shallow bay on the eastern side of the island. The troops were landed from fourteen destroyer transports, and before 7 A.M. the landing was complete and the destroyers pulled out.

The second echelon consisted of a dozen Landing Craft Infantry. They ran into trouble. The Japanese had been surprised again by the destroyer landing, and there had been no opposition, but by the time the LCIs came, so did six bombers and forty-eight Japanese fighter planes. There were several near misses but no hits, and the LCIs landed their troops and moved away.

The third wave of assault came in landing ship tanks, which had some difficulty getting near enough to shore to put down their ramps. Just after noon more Japanese attackers came. They were driven off by the antiaircraft gunners, who claimed to have shot down a half-dozen planes. That afternoon American planes from the air base in the Russell Islands raided Kahili airfield in Bougainville, and broke up an Eleventh Air Fleet effort to make a night attack on the Vella Lavella landing. A few planes came in that evening, but not many.

Soon the island was secured. The Japanese, facing a new, stringent policy of conserving men and equipment, decided to make no attempt to recapture this island, and also not to send any more reinforcements to the Central Solomons. The new defense perimeter was the line. Rabaul and Bougainville were important, and even Kolombangara, because there were so many Japanese there. But the move southerly islands were not important to Tokyo any longer.

By August 15, the Americans had 4600 men on Vella Lavella. The Japanese wanted only to use the island only as a barge staging point to move men out of Kolombangara, and they sent Rear Admiral Matsuji Ijuin down four destroyers to do just that. When Admiral Wilkinson learned of this, he sent three destroyers to counter the move. They reached Kolombangara before midnight of August 17, and encountered the Japanese.

Admiral Ijuin began by firing thirty-one torpedoes. But the American destroyers were not to be mouse-trapped. They maneuvered and all the torpedoes missed. The Americans opened fire, their five-inch guns directed by radar, and got a hit on the destroyer *Hamakaze*. As for the rest, it was maneuver, maneuver, maneuver, with no results—a good indication that the American destroyer men were becoming competitive with the Japanese. It seemed out of character for the Japanese destroyers to avoid a fight, but that was the order; they were to concentrate their efforts, not get drawn into such minor fracases. The Japanese destroyers had been escorting several barges, and these generally dispersed. The Americans did manage to hit two subchasers, two torpedo boats, and one *daihatsu*, but the most of them got away in the darkness. The engagement had to be recorded as nondecisive.

For the next few days, the Americans continued the buildup on Vella Lavella, and the Japanese responded only in the air, making bombing raids that damaged several LSTs and two destroyers. By October 1 the American and New Zealand troops of the Third Division had cornered the six hundred Japanese remaining on the island.

The Japanese were now withdrawing their much larger garrison from Kolombangara. They planned the withdrawal for the ten days in the dark of the moon. Admiral Wilkinson gussed they would do so, and he sent warships to prowl around the Slot until the night of September 25, when a Japanese submarine nearly torpedoed the cruiser *Columbia*. Still destroyers came back and kept sniping away at the *daihatsu* that were making regular runs from Kolombangara to Choiseul Island. As usual, the Japanese were doing a good job of evacuation, bringing thousands of men out of the threatened island.

These days, when the Japanese were short of destroyers, the American bases were bulging with them. On the night of September 29 no fewer than ten destroyers in three groups were snooping around the Slot. The destroyer *Eaton* sank the Japanese submarine *I-20* on the surface that night.

On October 2, two American destroyer groups had a brush

with four Japanese destroyers evacuating troops from Ko-lombangara. The Japanese *Samidare* was damaged, but the Japanese destroyers pulled away. They fired torpedoes, but it was obvious that they did not want to fight. Their orders were to evacuate troops, not lose destroyers in battle.

The Americans came down on Kolombangara again on the night of October 3, but they found very little because the Japanese had completed the evacuation of the island. They had taken off 10,000 men, proving again their skill in such operations, and proving that they really were still better ship handlers than the Americans at this stage of the war, despite the American radar.

So the Central Solomons campaign was virtually over. All that remained south of Choiseul were six hundred Japanese stranded on Vella Lavella, some of them survivors of ship actions. On the night of October 6, Admiral Ijuin came down to Vella Lavella to rescue these six hundred Japanese troops stranded there. He had nine destroyers when he left Rabaul but he picked up four submarine chasers, four PT boats, and four *daihatsu* to take with him. That night he sent three transport destroyers and two escorting destroyers to Marquana Bay on the northwest shore of Vella Lavella to begin the loading of the men.

On the afternoon of October 6, Admiral Wilkinson was informed of the movement of Japanese destroyers down toward the Slot. He had only three destroyers to send out, because all the others were engaged in convoy duty connected with the Americans buildup on Guadalcanal and New Georgia for the next steps in the move northward. Captain Frank Walker had the *Selfridge*, the *Chevalier*, and the *O'Bannon* off Choiseul Island. Admiral Wilkinson ordered him to Vella Lavella waters, and also detached three other destroyers from a convoy that was south of New Georgia. They were the *Ralph Talbot*, the *Taylor*, and the *Lavallette*.

So as dusk fell, six American destroyers were moving toward Marquana Bay to attack the Japanese. In the twilight the Japanese floatplanes, known generically to the Americans as "Washing Machine Charlie" because of the tinny sound of their engines, came out from their base at the Shortlands. The floatplanes began doing the job they did so well, keeping tabs on the Americans and their own ships, and protecting the latter by bombing and using flares to expose the American actions. Captain Walker moved his forces into a rainsquall but he had to come out, when he did, there was "Washing Machine Charlie," waiting.

Based on the radio intercepts and the breaking of the Japanese naval code, Wilkinson knew that Admiral Ijuin had nine destroyers and he knew where to go to attack. Captain Walker soon knew, too, and he wagered Captain Harold Larson, commander of the second contingent of American destroyers, that he would beat Larsen to Marquana Bay. So, with his eyes wide open, Captain Walker went in with three ships against the Japanese nine.

At about 10:30 the American radar picked up the Japanese ships in two groups, and Captain Walker charged in at 30 knots to attack. The destroyer transports, *Fumizuki*, *Matsukaze*, and *Yunagi*, pulled out, without their passengers, and headed back for safer waters. Admiral Ijuin set out to fight what he thought were a combination of cruisers and destroyers.

Four minutes after the Americans made contact by radar, the Japanese lookouts made contact with the enemy by eye, and soon the battle was joined. Captain Walker had won his bet. He called for Captain Larson, but Larson's three destroyers had not reached the bay yet.

Just before eleven P.M., when the Japanese were six miles away, Captain Walker attacked. The three destroyers launched fourteen torpedoes. Then they began to use gunfire. Admiral Ijuin was not alert and missed his chance to fire at this time, and it was four minutes before eleven P.M. when the *Yugumo* launched eight torpedoes. The *Yugumo* was closest to the Americans, so she drew their gunfire while the other Japanese destroyers did not.

At 11:01, just as the *Chevalier* was turning her machine guns on a Japanese PT boat, she was rocked by an explosion. One of the *Yugumo*'s torpedoes had hit. Seconds later, the *O'Bannon*, next in line, smashed into the starboard side of the stricken destroyer.

At 11:05, an enormous explosion shook the *Yugumo* and she flared up like a torch. An American torpedo had struck. Other American ships were firing on her, and she soon went down.

Heated by the chase, Captain Walker set out in the *Selfridge* alone after the *Shigure* and the *Samidare*, not sure that Admiral Ijuin would fight. But he soon got his answer when sixteen torpedoes boiled around his destroyer. The helmsman combed through several wakes, but one torpedo struck and the ship came to a quick dead stop.

By this time, about 11:15, "Washing Machine Charlie" had reported to Admiral Ijuin that three more "cruisers" were coming. This was Larson's destroyer force. When Ijuin learned that he would face more cruisers, he decided to retire, and gave the order to head back for Rabaul. The destroyer transports were waiting off the Shortlands to resume their rescue mission, but their help was not necessary. Under the cover of the flight, the subchasers had moved into Marquana Bay, taken off the 589 waiting Japanese, and sailed for Buin.

That night the *Chevalier* was sunk by a torpedo fired from the *LaVallette*. The *Selfridge* was struggling to stay afloat, and Captain Walker together with most of the crew, was taken off by the *Taylor*. The crippled *Selfridge* and *O'Bannon* were then escorted back to Purvis Bay by the three destroyers of Captain Larson's group.

As morning came, all that was left in the waters of the battle were the *O'Bannon*'s lifeboats, left behind for stray survivors. One of them was commandeered by three officers and twenty-two men from the *Yugumo*, and made it back to Japanese territory in this gift boat. American PT boats picked up seventy-eight Japanese survivors but one of them showed Americans why never to do it again. That Japanese, remembering too well the tenets of the new Bushido, killed a PT boat sailor on *PT 163* while the sailor was giving him a cup of coffee!

Next day both sides claimed great victory. Captain Walker said he had destroyed three enemy destroyers and damaged several others. Admiral Ijuin claimed to have sunk two cruisers and three destroyers. So the "morale" victory was shared by the two.

But the fact was that the Japanese had won again. Although the Americans had displayed that new-found skill with their torpedoes and a newly aggressive attitude, the Japanese had sunk one destroyer, badly damaged another, and caused a third to collide with the first, doing yet more damage. The Japanese cost had been just one destroyer. And the Japanese rescue mission was a complete success.

Despite that Japanese victory, it was apparent that the war had turned around. The Central Solomons campaign of the Allies had taken from February to October 1943. After the I Operation in April, the Japanese had been on the defensive constantly. The war since Guadalcanal had cost them seventeen warships, as compared to the Americans' six. It had also cost the Japanese hundreds of aircraft and pilots on a ratio of at least three Japanese to one Allied flier. The Americans now held Guadalcanal, the Russells, the New Georgia group, Vella Lavella, and Kolombangara.

In another sense, too, it was a brand-new war in the Pacific. Until the summer of 1943 Admiral Nimitz and General MacArthur had operated "on a shoestring," but with the successful invasion of North Africa and the movement into Italy, the American high command had relaxed a little and the amount of war material available in the Pacific was increasing every day. As the official American naval historian Samuel Eliot Morison put it, "Henceforth the United States Navy would conduct the Pacific War with mass production methods."

That was the change. The Japanese were brave and tough, but their country had a population only half the size of the United States', and Japan's industrial power was at a virtual standstill. She could not even replace the warships lost in the South Pacific struggle, while the Americans were shuttling ships from the ways to the embattled seas day by day. By the fall of 1943 there was no way the Japanese could win the war, and even General Tojo was beginning to suspect the truth, although he still clung desperately to his hope that a victory in China would bring about an "honorable settlement" of the war in the Pacific.

CHAPTER TWENTY-ONE

Bougainville Assault

Until September 1943, the Americans were planning to move from New Georgia into the Shortlands for the next invasion up the chain of the Solomons Islands. The Shortlands were a major Japanese base for destroyer operations and seaplanes. But for some time the Joint Chiefs of Staff had been thinking how wasteful it was to just keep moving up one island at a time. The Shortlands was a long way from Rabaul, and its capture would do nothing to hasten the day of isolating Rabaul. Moreover, in the fighting for Munda, the Allies had learned how desperately the Japanese would defend their installations. What they wanted were airfields from which they could bomb Rabaul and keep that base from supplying others.

At one point General MacArthur had considered a frontal attack on Rabaul, which everyone knew would be very expensive in terms of aircraft, ships, and men. But after the capture of Lae and Salamaua in the early fall of 1943,* MacArthur had changed his mind too, and by September everyone had agreed that such spots as the Shortlands and even Choiseul, with its thousands of troops in occupation, could safely be bypassed. The key island in the Solomons was Bougainville, because from this island planes could easily reach New Britain and bomb Rabaul.

*See *The Jungles of New Guinea*, volume No. 4 in this series.

Bougainville was a big island, and it was stoutly defended by more than a division of Japanese army troops, plus several thousand naval troops manning airfields and sea bases. So the plan was further refined: the Americans would not try to capture Bougainville outright, but would select a portion of the island suitable for air base construction and set up an invasion perimeter. To find the right place, the Americans sent a number of small survey parties to Bougainville. They were careless, and dropped K-ration boxes and other obviously American remnants at their bivouack areas, so the Japanese knew that Bougainville was a target for invasion. But fortunately several parties had been sent to several locations, and so, in the fall of 1943, the Japanese did not know exactly where the Americans planned to land. Since Bougainville is 130 miles long and 30 miles wide there were plenty of places.

The Japanese on Bougainville were mostly in the south and in the north, and their bases were not connected because there was no road that ran the length of the island, only trails that ran along the ridges of the north-south range, the Crown Prince Mountains.

The Japanese Army Sixth Division had its headquarters and 15,000 men around the Kieta, Kahili, and Kara airfields in the south. In the north there were perhaps 10,000 army and navy troops, around Buka and Buin airfields and at naval installations. Altogether, there were about 40,000 army and navy personnel on the island, and they were well-equipped for defense, so it would have been extremely expensive, indeed, to try an all-out frontal assault. Besides, the Americans really wanted only the airfield positions. So, after survey, one of the least prepossessing areas of Bougainville appeared to be the proper spot for invasion: Empress Augusta Bay and Cape Torokina on the southwest coast of the island, which were inaccessible to the Japanese positions in south and north. Only about three thousand Japanese were stationed in this whole big area of central Bougainville and their communication with north and south was either over trails by foot or by barge and small boat over the sea.

On August 21, Admiral Wilkinson sent a party of marine raiders in the submarine *Greenling* to the Treasury Islands to look over Blanche Harbor, which he thought would be a good position for a radar station. Later reconnaissance parties brought back information that the Treasury Islands were occupied by only about 250 men. So on October 27, destroyer transports landed more than six thousand troops, mostly New Zealanders, around Blanche Harbor.

At the same time destroyer transports landed a raiding force of 725 Marines from the Second Marine Parachute Battalion on Choiseul Island. It was commanded by Lieutenant Colonel Victor Krulak. The troops made a feint of invading, by attacking Choiseul Island, and raided a Japanese post at Sangigai, where a thousand soldiers recently taken off Kolombangara were encamped. They destroyed the base for barges there, and then they withdrew.

All this activity had convinced the Japanese that the Allies' next invasion point would be the Shortlands, and they acted accordingly. They looked for invasion at the south end of Bougainville.

At this point the Japanese were heavily embroiled in battle. General MacArthur was moving against Finschhafen in New Guinea and threatened their whole position on that island. The airfields of Rabaul were under almost constant assault by the Fifth Air Force, which was moving bases closer and closer to Rabaul. Indeed, the major thrust of MacArthur's New Guinea campaign was the securing of sites for new air bases with which to ring Rabaul. And now came this new threat from the southern Solomons.

The Allies faced a particularly vexing problem in invading Bougainville. The Japanese had come to the island early in 1942 and been greeted warmly there by German missionaries, since Germany was Japan's ally. Bougainville was not administratively a part of the Solomons Islands, but had its own administrative system, under a special League of Nations mandate to Australia. It was in almost every way separate from the other islands in the group, and retained a greater share of German influence. The Germans helped the Japanese to round up the Australians and other foreigners with Allied connections, and by dint of good treatment the Bougainville natives, unlike the other Solomon islanders, had been converted to a pro-Japanese and anti-Allies stance.

For a time Allied coast watchers operated on Bougainville, but in the heart of the Guadalcanal campaign the Japanese had conducted a strong drive against them, and all the survivors had been withdrawn. For months the coast watchers had been arguing that they could function on Bougainville despite Japanese vigilance and the unfriendliness of the natives there, and had been agitating to return to Bougainville. So, at the end of October, the submarine *Guardfish* delivered one Australian party to the south end of the island, and one to the north.

As October neared its end, the Japanese knew that something important was stirring. Earlier, Admiral Koga had believed it was the invasion of Wake Island, and had moved the Combined Fleet down to Eniwetok, prepared to fight the decisive battle with the American Pacific Fleet. But that fleet did not appear, and so Koga had gone back to Truk. The American movement, the Japanese leaders decided, was going to come in the Solomons, probably around Choiseul and the Shortlands. So Koga dispatched the aircraft of his carriers *Zuikaku*, *Shokaku*, and *Zuiho*—nearly 175 strong—to Rabaul to strengthen the Eleventh Air Fleet, and also ordered the Twelfth Air Fleet in Japan to be prepared to move to Rabaul.

The air battle for Rabaul was furious. On October 12, the Fifth Air Force sent 349 planes against Rabaul. On October 18, they sent another big raid, but only about fifty bombers got through the bad weather. They came back with exorbitant claims of damage to the Japanese that did not fool the Japanese, but did convince MacArthur's staff, that Rabaul was about half-knocked-out. The contrary was true: Rabaul had at that moment at least two hundred planes available. On October 23, 24, and 25 General Kenney's Fifth Air Force staged new Rabaul raids, and claimed to have shot down 175 planes. Again the pilots were seeing things; the Japanese losses reported were thirty-four destroyed, mostly on the ground, and twenty-seven damaged. Again on October 29 the Fifth Air Force raided and again claimed big damage: forty-five planes destroyed and much bomb damage to installations. Not so, said the Japanese: ten planes destroyed and little damage to installations.

In the last days of October the weather was too foul for

raids on Rabaul. On November 1, the Japanese carrier planes arrived, which brought the Rabaul air force up to strength, and on November 2, when the Fifth Air Force came back with seventy-five B-25 bombers and eighty P-38 fighters, they were met with a very powerful defense. Again the Allied claims were excessive. But for that matter, so were the Japanese claims.

The Americans claimed to have shot down eighty-five Japanese planes and probably to have shot down twenty-three more or 113 in all, and to have hit 114,000 tons of shipping in that raid. The Japanese said it was twenty planes downed and three ships, or 5100 tons sunk. But the Japanese claimed twenty-two B-25s and seventy-nine of the eighty P-38s, when the actual losses were nine bombers and ten fighters. So while one could believe what the air forces said about numbers of planes sent out on missions and numbers that returned, one really could not believe much of anything the airmen said as to the numbers of enemy planes destroyed—and of course the reason for exaggeration on both sides was the same: pride and excitement.

Gearing up for the new Allied movement they expected in the Solomons, the Japanese announced Operation RO, which was to be a new strong effort of the Rabaul air force against enemy naval forces and enemy air forces in New Guinea and the Solomons area. The Japanese air raids became more persistent than they had been for months, and were executed with greater air strength, although not with as much skill as before. The number of Japanese planes actually shot down in this period kept increasing, a tribute to the growing skill of the Allied antiaircraft gunners and airmen, but equally a commentary on the lessening reserve of skilled Japanese airmen. It was becoming the naval air force's greatest problem, and the so-called "cooperation" between army and navy air forces had already proved to be mostly talk. The naval air forces were still carrying the air war in the South Pacific.

The invasion of Bougainville presented special problems for the Americans, but some of them at least were made less serious by the Allies. At Pearl Harbor Admiral Nimitz was planning an invasion of the Gilberts Islands with Admiral Raymond Spruance's Fifth Fleet, and since this invasion involved a long trek across the Central Pacific to hit enemy-held beaches, it demanded plenty of punch. Thus, for his Bougainville invasion, Admiral Halsey would initially have only one carrier group and one cruiser division, plus a number of destroyers under Commander Arleigh Burke, who had just been fleeted up to be a captain. The ground forces would consist of the I Marine Amphibious Corps, reinforced, under Lieutenant General Alexander Vandegrift, who had been the initial commander at Guadalcanal. He had the Third Marine Division, reinforced, the Thirty-seventh U.S. Army Infantry Division, and, from the New Zealanders, the Eighth Brigade Group of the Third New Zealand Division, plus Advance Naval Base Unit No. 7. They would be delivered to Empress Augusta Bay in twelve APAs and AKAs (military transport and cargo ships), plus such smaller vessels as Admiral Wilkinson could put together from his Guadalcanal force.

The big problem for the landings, Admiral Wilkinson knew, would be the closeness of the Japanese sources of air power—all those airfields in north and south Bougainville and in the Shortlands. He did not know of the coming of Operation RO, but he might have expected some such super effort by the Japanese, and the landing site was only 210 miles from Rabaul. Wilkinson's basic air support would come from Airsols—a new command in the Solomons that employed army, navy, and marine corps planes. Just then, in October 1943, the headquarters had been moved to Munda to bring it up forward for the invasion. The forward air base was at Vella Lavella, where three marine air squadrons were assigned to cover the Bougainville operation.

All during October Airsols had been harrying the Japanese at Kahili, Kara, Ballale, Bonis, and Buka airfields, on or near Bougainville, and 158 different missions had been flown, or 3259 individual plane sorties. Some Japanese planes were destroyed—not as many as claimed, of course—but the real value of the missions was to keep Japanese heads down, and to keep their shipment of aircraft to this vital area at a minimum. The official U.S. naval history says the airfields were pulverized. That was not quite so; it was very difficult to pulverize an airfield, as the Americans knew from their experience at Henderson Field at

Guadalcanal. But the result of all the Allied air activity was that the Japanese had to make extensive use of their techniques of camouflage and concealment of planes.

How the odds had changed! On November 1 the Japanese had perhaps three hundred planes in the area, but the Americans at Airsols had nearly five hundred, plus the carrier forces, the bombers and reconnaissance planes of Admiral Fitch, and the indirect support of the Fifth Air Force, which kept pasting Rabaul.

As the invasion time came near, Admiral Halsey also directed some bombardment missions for Bougainville. Admiral Merrill's Task Force 39, with four light cruisers and Destroyer Squadron 23, headed for Buka Passage on October 31 and bombarded the Buka and Bonis airfields in the early hours of the morning. Then the force moved at 30 knots to the Shortlands to bombard there as well.

On D Day November 1, the Bougainville invasion force had the help of more air power from Rear Admiral Frederick C. Sherman's task group from Task Force 38, which had come down with the carriers *Saratoga* and *Princeton.** Admiral Sherman's carriers came in and struck the Buka Passage airfields on November 1 and 2.

On November 1 the invasion force moved toward Cape Torokina. It was charted water, but not very well charted. The German Admiralty had done the job about 1890, when Bougainville was a German colony, but they had not done it right, and there were many unknown reefs and shoals in the area. The beach curved around the bay, and behind it was the jungle, and behind that the mountain range, with a smoking volcano, Mount Bagana, at 8500 feet.

Although there were an estimated three hundred Japanese troops on the shores of the bay, there were fewer than that in the area where the Americans landed. As everyone concerned knew, the real problem was not the landing, but what would come after, when Rabaul's airmen were apprised of the landing. Admiral Wilkinson had emphasized before that

---

*An indication of the new power of the American navy was the carrier force. In November 1943, the Pacific Fleet and its subsidiaries had available four carrier groups, comprising eleven fleet carriers and light carriers and two escort carrier groups comprising eight smaller carriers. Most of these were required for the invasion of the Gilberts on November 10, but there was plenty of air power to go around.

the main objective was to get in, get the troops ashore, and get the ships out in a hurry before the air attacks began.

Fourteen thousand troops were making this landing, and eight thousand of them went in in the first wave, very smoothly, despite fire from the shore that sank four landing craft and damaged ten others, costing seventy men. The gun that did the damage was knocked out by a single marine, Sergeant Robert Owens, who charged into the bunker and drove the Japanese gunners out into the guns of his friends. But Owens himself was shot down and his body was riddled with bullets.

Most of the damage was caused by that one 75-mm gun on Cape Torokina. But more dangerous was the surf, and about eighty-five landing craft were stranded on the beaches once they had landed the troops because the approaches were so steep that the landing craft swung around at the deep end and broached.

The marines moved inland on two narrow corridors of dry land in the swampy ground and began flushing out Japanese. They had snipers and dogs to find the enemy snipers, and by nightfall the last Japanese pillbox in the area was knocked out.

The first wave of marines hit the beach just before 7:30 A.M. The first Japanese air attack came about five minutes later. Admiral Wilkinson ordered the transports to get moving and get out of there, as nine bombers and forty-four Zeroes came in to work over the ships and the beaches. For some reason only sixteen American planes showed up to defend against this attack, but they prevented the Japanese from doing any serious damage.

The next attack came at one o'clock in the afternoon and this one was more serious, involving about one hundred aircraft, most of them from the carriers which had been sent down to Rabaul. But thirty-four Airsols fighter planes showed up to frustrate the Japanese. One transport ran aground and was a sitting duck, but the fighters protected her, and two tugs labored mightily to get her off.

By 5:30 in the afternoon eight of the twelve ships involved in the landing were unloaded and the 14,000 men and 6200 tons of supplies were ashore. The four others started out to sea, were called back because their supplies would be needed, and then, when an enemy air and sea attack was announced, were sent to sea again.

That night the Japanese cruisers came down towards Bougainville to disrupt the landings, as all the Allied commanders involved knew they would do. It was reminiscent of the Savo Island battle at the opening of the siege of Guadalcanal. But the Americans of November 1943 were not the Americans of August 1942.

CHAPTER TWENTY-TWO

Admiral Omori Attacks

Admiral Koga was looking for a chance to hit the Americans hard, but he had to be careful for two reasons: first because of his shortage of fuel, and second, because of the need to escort valuable convoys with capital ships because Japanese destroyers were such short in supply these days. Admiral Sentaro Omori had brought a convoy of transports down from Truk to Rabaul on October 30, so he was on hand at Rabaul when word came of the cruiser force (Admiral Merrill's) moving to bombard the airfields at the southern end of Bougainville. Admiral Koga gave orders that Omori was to move out and hit the cruiser force.

Koga's instructions were all well and good, but the South Pacific is a big area, and Admiral Omori missed connections with the Americans, so his mission was in vain. He turned toward Rabaul in the small hours of November 1.

By noon on November 1, when Admiral Omori pulled into Simpson Harbor, Admiral Samejima, commander of the Eight Fleet, had a new mission waiting for him: to take a counterlanding force in five destroyer transports and oppose the American landings at Bougainville. Once again the Japanese army authorities completely misread the signs. The Americans had put 14,000 men ashore at Empress Augusta Bay that day; the Japanese landing force was to be a thousand troops.

So at five P.M. that day, as the American transports prepared to move out of Empress Augusta Bay—at least for the night, which was expected to be full of aerial fire-works—Admiral Omori sailed from Rabaul. With him were the heavy cruisers *Myoko* and *Haguro*, the light cruisers, *Sendai* and *Agano*, and six destroyers. Outside, in St. George's Channel, he was supposed to meet the loaded transport destroyers, but they were not there. As Omori waited, his lookouts reported an enemy submarine, and then the *Sendai* was narrowly missed by a bomb. Admiral Omori felt very insecure out here in these waters, waiting. When the destroyer transports showed up, he learned that they could not make more than 26 knots, which made them a definite liability in a struggle with American cruisers and modern destroyers. So Admiral Omori suggested that he go on with the cruiser force and attack the American transports at Bougainville, and that the counterlanding be delayed until he had done that. Admiral Samejima acceded and so Omori headed for Bougainville at 32 knots.

As he sped along, he was shadowed by two American army reconnaissance planes, which sent the word to Admiral Halsey's command. Admiral Merrill was informed. He had the cruisers *Montpelier, Cleveland, Columbia,* and *Denver*. He also had four destroyers under Captain Arleigh Burke and four more under Commander B. L. Austin. The cruisers and Austin's destroyers were off Vella Lavella, but Burke's force was down at the head of Kula Gulf refuelling. Admiral Merrill set a meeting point off Empress Augusta Bay, and set out with two-thirds of his force. Burke hurried to catch up.

At last the Americans had evolved a destroyer strategy to deal with the Japanese. In the past the destroyers had been tied to the tails of the large ships, but on this night Commander Austin's destroyers were positioned fore and aft of the cruiser line. It was understood that when they made contact with the enemy they were free to attack with torpedoes and not wait for an order to begin firing their guns.

After midnight the Japanese and American forces began to draw together. At 1:30 in the morning Admiral Omori's force had its first contact with the enemy when a plane flew over the force and dropped a bomb, striking the heavy cruiser *Haguro* and damaging her enough to slow her to 30 knots. The whole formation cut speed.

At 1:40 an observation floatplane from the *Haguro* reported sighting a cruiser and three destroyers fifty miles away. This was a part of the American force. The Japanese changed course to find the Americans, and then another plane reported ships in Empress Augusta Bay. The report said they were transports, but the transports were outside, inside were minelayers, which had laid a mine field north of Cape Torokina.

Admiral Merrill's force slowed to 20 knots, so that the ships' wakes would not attract the attention of the Japanese observation planes, and headed toward the enemy. The admiral laid his ships out in front of the entrance to Empress Augusta Bay, and proposed to let the destroyers launch torpedoes first. This was all quite unlike previous American plans for battle.

At 2:27 that morning the American radar made contact with the enemy ships. By that time Captain Burke's destroyers had shown up, and they were detached to make a torpedo attack. Two minutes later Admiral Merrill turned the cruisers around, putting the rear destroyers in front; they had instructions to deliver a torpedo attack as well.

At 2:45 one of those skillful Japanese floatplane pilots dropped a flare over Admiral Merrill's cruisers and lit up the area. The lookouts aboard the light cruiser *Sendai* spotted the scene, and Admiral Omori turned to close with his enemies.

At 2:46 Captain Burke's destroyers, which were coming up on the northern flank of the Japanese, launched torpedoes and turned away to the right.

At 2:50 the Japanese northern columns of ships—the *Sendai*, *Shigure*, *Samidare*, and *Shiratsuyu*—fired torpedoes at the cruisers and Commander Austin's destroyers. As they turned, the *Sendai* column of ships fired eight torpedoes at the Americans.

At 2:51 Admiral Merrill ordered his ships to begin gunfire against the enemy. *Sendai* was the target, and she took numerous hits from the various American ships, all firing by radar. The *Sendai* began to burn. The destroyers *Samidare* and *Shiratsuyu* collided while turning to avoid the cruiser fire, but because of their turn, all of Captain Burke's destroyers' torpedoes missed.

The Americans made smoke to get out of view of the enemy, and the *Myoko* and *Haguro* turned south. The American gunnery was much improved this night, and the destroyer *Hatsukaze*, trying to avoid fire, collided with the cruiser *Myoko*, which added to the Japanese confusion.

Admiral Merrill kept his cruisers constantly in motion, thus ruining Japanese plans to make torpedo attacks on them, but with their radar, even while zigzagging at 30 knots, they were able to keep trained on the enemy and keep firing. But if the American gunnery this night was vastly improved, one could not say the same of the quality of the American munitions. The Japanese cruiser *Haguro* was hit six times, but four of the six-inch shells were duds which did about as much damage as a large rock.

The Japanese gunnery was good. Soon eight-inch shells were hitting the leading American cruiser, the *Denver*. But the Japanese were having munitions trouble too, and three eight-inch shells that struck the forward part of the *Denver* did not explode, but passed through the hull, letting in a lot of water.

At 3:26, when the cruiser forces were about seven miles apart, enemy planes again illuminated the Americans with flares. The flares and star shells gave a false impression, and Admiral Omori believed that he had sunk two of the cruisers, so he disengaged at 3:37. Captain Burke's destroyers found the *Hatsukaze*, which had already been badly damaged by the destroyer *Spence*, and helped sink her.

The destroyer *Foote* ran into one of the Japanese torpedoes fired at the cruisers. It blew her stern off and she stopped, right in front of the *Spence*, which then sideswiped the *Thatcher*. The *Spence* also took an enemy shell, which spilled water into her fuel supply and caused her to slow down.

The American force now suffered from a good deal of confusion, which prevented it from getting at the Japanese cruisers. The *Sendai* which was about half-sunk, was hit by American torpedoes, but she was still afloat when Captain Burke came along and fired at her with his five-inch guns.

Whether by torpedoes or by guns, or by torpedoes *and* guns, the *Sendai* was finally sunk.

At 4:54 Admiral Merrill ordered all his destroyers to close on the flagship. Admiral Merrill felt that dawn would bring new air attacks and he wanted his force together and available to protect the transports. How right he was. Just after five o'clock in the morning the first air strike from Rabaul arrived, even though flying weather in the area was so bad that the Airsols protective fighters from Vella Lavella did not get into the air in time to help. But eight Allied planes (four New Zealand Warhawks) did arrive and drove off the Japanese before they could reach the cruisers. They claimed to have shot down eight planes.

The major Japanese air strike of the morning, more than 100 planes, arrived to attack the cruisers. It ignored the destroyers. By furious maneuvering, Admiral Merrill's ships kept out of trouble until two bombs hit the *Montpelier*, but they killed only one man and did not do vital damage to the ship.

The second air raid planned by Rabaul for that day never got off the ground, because General Kenney's Fifth Air Force staged a big raid on the Rabaul airfields, keeping the planes on the ground.

That day, November 2, the four transports that had not been unloaded on D Day were unloaded at Empress Augusta Bay. The cruiser force then escorted the four transports until the morning of November 3, when they met the cruiser *Nashville* and the destroyer *Pringle* which had come up from Guadalcanal, and took over the escort duty.

The battle of Empress Augusta Bay ended with almost as much damage done to the various ships by collisions as by gunfire. It was an American victory, but not a conclusive or tidy one; Admiral Omori thought he had won by sinking at least two cruisers.

And as for the Bougainville landings, the Battle of Empress Augusta Bay had contributed little other than that, by being on the scene, Admiral Merrill had obviously saved the four transports that had not finished their unloading. But while all this was going on, Admiral Koga had reinforced Admiral Samejima's Eighth Fleet at Rabaul with seven heavy cruisers, a light cruiser, and several destroyers. So there was bound to be more action at sea within the next few hours.

When the first wave of marines landed at Cape Torokina at 7:26 on the morning of November 1, they moved onto twelve separate beaches. The Japanese, 270 strong, were dug in with eighteen pillboxes to protect their entrenched positions. One Japanese platoon with several heavy machine guns on Puruata Island, and a squad was located on Torokina Island. The Japanese had positioned their 75 mm-gun on the northwest end of Cape Torokina.

The Japanese had chosen their positions with their usual skill, and as the boats came in line with Puruata Island, they found themselves under crossfire from three points. The boats sped in, taking casualties, but there were so many boats—carrying 14,000 marines—that the effect seemed almost negligable. But by the time the boats got inside and onto the beach, the 75-mm gun had done a great deal of damage. Take Boat No. 21 from the transport *President Adams*. It was hit by three shells from the 75-mm gun. The first shell killed the navy coxwain, sending the boat out of control. The second and third shells killed the boat's two officers and twelve men, as well as wounding fourteen other men.

That single 75-mm gun did so much damage to the landing that the whole enterprise became disorganized until Sergeant Owens went after it single-handedly. His heroic action cannot be said to have made the difference between success or failure of the invasion, but it was in the highest traditions of the Marine Corps.

Between broaching boats, turning over on the steep shores of several beaches, and enemy fire, it was not an easy landing, although the result was never really in doubt. What was really remarkable was the ability of the 270 defenders to keep 14,000 marines off balance for most of a day. By nightfall the marines were in full control of the situation. By noon of the second day they had eliminated almost all the Japanese, and the surviving troops had fallen back into the jungle ridge line not far from the west bank of the Piva River.

On this second morning, as the marines examined the terrain into which they had moved, they saw that they were in a potential trap. Except for two solid land lines to Cape Torokina, the whole area was swampy ground and jungle so thick that the marines had to hack their way through. They discovered one trail that led to the Japanese position, and they blocked that. Then they sent patrols out to probe from the beach to the mountains. It was very slow going. But they persevered, and by the third day the seabees had come in and started building the roads that would lead to the airstrips up on solid ground. First to be built would be a fighter strip, then a bomber field. But that meant capturing more high ground, and then building a defensive perimeter around it. It was not going to be easy to defend this enclave in the middle of a Japanese-held island. But that was what must be done, for the purpose of the invasion was to create a site for the Allied aircraft to attack Rabaul and keep it on the defensive from then on.

On the second day, the beachhead was established to a depth of over a mile. On the third day, the marines began to bury the dead Japanese; they found 192 bodies. Up on the ridge the Japanese counted noses. Only 78 of their garrison had survived. But Rabaul had promised reinforcement, and they were soon to be in touch with the Sixth Division, 15,000 strong, in the south.

The American position was extremely tenuous, especially if the Japanese chose to exercise a major movement such as an attack by the Sixth Division from the south, which could be brought around by landing craft in an amphibious operation. Admiral Wilkinson had no way of knowing whether or not the Japanese were capable of such a move. He did not understand, that one of the great weaknesses of the Japanese enemies was their consistent underestimation of the Allied enemy.

The second and third days of the invasion were spent in consolidating the marine positions. The Japanese strength, what there was of it, was on the west, and General A.H. Turnage moved the Third Marines to that side, and put the Ninth marines further out. To the left of the marines, west of Torokina, was the Laruma River; on the their right flank was the Piva River; and up in back were the mountain mass and the volcano, smoking ominously.

* * *

When Admiral Koga at Truk learned that Admiral Omori had failed to deal a knockout blow to the invaders at Empress Augusta Bay, he hurried his heavy cruisers, a light cruiser, and four destroyers to Rabaul for the new strike planned in connection with the RO Operation in the air. On the way south, Allied planes bombed the oilers *Nichiei Maru* and *Nissho Maru*. These which had to be towed back to Truk for repairs, putting a serious crimp in Koga's oil supply system. And on November 4, as the troopships set out from Rabaul to reinforce the Japanese on Bougainville, they were beset by B-24 bombers from New Guinea. That assault resulted in one damaged transport having to be towed back to Rabaul for repairs, and put a big hole in the reinforcement program.

At Rabaul Admiral Samejima was making plans for use of the big cruiser force that sat in Simpson Harbor on the morning of November 5. At Noumea Admiral Halsey had some plans for those cruisers too. He still had the use of Admiral Sherman's two-carrier task group for a few days, and he sent Sherman to make an air strike against the eight heavy cruisers and light cruisers and destroyers. This was a very bold move, particularly since it was known that the Japanese air power on Rabaul had just recently been beefed up.

At nine A.M. on November 5, Admiral Sherman launched ninety-seven planes from his two carriers—forty-five of them bombers and the rest, fighters. They flew on in perfect weather, little cloud and plenty of sunshine and blue sky; fifty miles from Rabaul they could see the big ships clustered in the harbor.

Commander Henry Caldwell, leader of the air strike, was worried about the Japanese defenses. All these cruisers and destroyers bristled with antiaircraft guns, and he had to expect a swarm of fighters to come up to meet the attack. He kept a tight formation, fighters on top, which did not break until the point of attacks, when dive-bombers went one way and torpedo bombers another.

The Japanese fighters, which were in the air and approaching, waited too long to intercept, and when they did attack, found themselves facing Japanese antiaircraft fire as well as the Americans'. As for the Japanese cruisers, they were caught completely by surprise. Some of them had been in harbor only for a few hours. One was fuelling.

The American planes screamed down through the flak. One bomb hit the heavy cruiser *Mogami*. The armor-piercing bomb penetrated below the second deck and started fires as it sped down into the engine room. There were sixty casualties among the men, and the cruiser itself was a casualty; she would have to go home to Japan for repairs. The cruiser *Maya* took a bomb down her main smokestack, which ended up in the engine room. She, too, had to be towed back to Truk. The cruiser *Takao* was hit twice, making it another candidate for dry-dock. Three near misses damaged the cruiser *Atago*, and bombs knocked out the forward turret on the light cruiser *Agano*. The light cruiser *Noshiro* and the destroyer *Fujinami* were both hit by dud torpedoes, and the destroyer *Wakatsuki* was damaged by bombs.

It was not a spectacular attack, and no ships were sunk this day. But the assault completely changed the plans of Admiral Koga. No longer did he have a cruiser force available to assault the Empress Augusta Bay landings.

The American losses were not inconsiderable—five fighter planes and five bombers—but when one considers that they were attacking the heart of Japan's southern base system, the losses were not exorbitant, either. Halsey had taken a risk and it had paid off. That same day Samejima's once-proud cruiser force upped anchor, several ships under tow, and headed for the safety of Truk.

That was Admiral Samejima's lost chance. At Truk Admiral Koga was aware of preparations for a new American assault in the Central Pacific. Almost immediately he would be so busy with the defense of the Gilberts Islands that he would have little time to consider the problems of Bougainville.

CHAPTER TWENTY-THREE

The Fight for Bougainville

When Admiral Halsey decided to move into Bougainville—knowing that a whole Japanese division occupied the whole southern part of the island—he was taking a calculated risk. He was betting that the communications problems of the Japanese would be so severe that he need not worry about that Sixth Division's presence so close by. But he did not *know* that, he surmised it, and in a way he was wrong. General Imamaura had advised General Hyukatake of the Seventeenth Army that the move was coming and asked him to oppose it. But as was so usual in the South Pacific campaign, the Japanese underestimated their enemy and sent a regiment to do something that would have required a division.

When the reinforcement of Bougainville by sea was delayed at Rabaul, Seventeenth Army headquarters got in touch with the Sixth Division in southern Bougainville and asked that the division lend a hand. The division headquarters then called on Colonel Shunaki Hamanoue, commander of the Twenty-third Regiment, who decided to send 2400 troops and to lead them himself to put an end to the Allied threat. Again it was a case of too little too late by the Japanese. Colonel Hamanoue actually only set out with three-hundred riflemen with mortars and machine guns. He made arrangements for supplies: the engineers were to send four *daihatsu* barges up to the Piva River entrance and the colonel's force would have plenty of supply. But the Airsols air force found those *daihatsu* on the morning of November 4, and sank all four of them. So Colonel Hamanoue and his men marched along with three days of iron rations and nothing else.

There was a way to go over the trails along the ridge, and it would take the colonel two days to make it, so he planned his attack for November 6. Hamanoue had some maps of this section of Bougainville, but they were of no more use than the German charts the Americans had collected. The colonel and his men found themselves stumbling along in hip-deep water, crossing swamps and small streams that were not on the maps. They got to the mouth of the Jaba River and discovered that it was both too deep to wade, and full of crocodiles. During the crossing a crocodile took one Japanese soldier. That ended the swimming of the river. They waited until the engineers produced some small rubber boats.

Then came more rivers, more swamps, more exhaustion and hunger. Colonel Hamanoue was half-discouraged even before he reached the jumping-off place near the shore, where he was to meet the first thousand troops of the counterlanding force being sent from Rabaul. This was the No. 2 Ken Butai, a unit of shock troops with much experience on the China front—where they did not have crocodiles.

The arrival of the troops from Rabaul was delayed, and delayed again. Finally the ships arrived off Empress Augusta Bay on the evening of November 6, but laid over until morning to land. They landed in three sections on the beach held by Company K of the Ninth Marines—altogether about 850 men with machine guns and a field gun. They dug in quickly as the marines attacked. The marines were slowed down by the jungle, and finally were pinned down and then withdrawn, covered by the First Battalion of the Third Marines. The fighting was very fierce, but the marines fought well. Still, the Japanese captured the west side of the beach that day, from the Laruma River to a point a mile away. They also cut off a platoon of Company B of the Third Marines. But the platoon set up a perimeter and guarded it through the night. Next morning they made it back to the marine lines.

The seaborne counterlanding was supposed to drive through the American line to reach Colonel Hamanoue's troops, but it did not make it. Instead it was pinned down on the beach area. When General Imamura learned of the plight of this first detachment and got some inkling of the numbers of Americans involved, he called off the second echelon, and the additional 2500 troops did not come to Bougainville.

Colonel Hamanoue was bivouacked on the east side of the Piva River, and moved along adjacent to the Piva trail, the only good trail that led to the mountains. His intent was to attack simultaneously with the troops from the beach and drive a wedge through the American line. But his plan did not work, and on the afternoon of November 7, the colonel retreated to a point west of Piva village. Next day he attacked again, and the result was the same. A few hundred men really did not have a chance against thousands. The Japanese problem was bad planning and bad intelligence more than bad execution. Colonel Hamanoue's men fought valiantly, breaking through the marine lines here and there, but always those lines closed up again, and the marines had the advantage of artillery which could set up a powerful barrage along the trail.

Between November 6 and November 10, the No. 2 Ken Butai struggled in the beach area, and on the 10th the remnants of the unit managed to fight their way to the Biba River landing. But Colonel Hamanoue's troops just seem to have disappeared on November 8. The Americans went up the Piva trail, expecting to be ambushed, but there were no Japanese around. The deciding factor was an artillery barrage on November 9 that had virtually wiped out the Japanese heavy weapons section. Since it would take a full week to get a new supply of guns and ammunition up to this front line, Colonel Hamanoue saw no recourse but to fall back or be wiped out. In spite of what was said about the Japanese in the war, such men as Colonel Hamanoue were not fools, and they did not throw away their lives or those of their men needlessly. Except in totally desperate and hopeless situations, senior officers did not advocate the "banzai" charges that usually meant death.

So by November 10 the marines held the Piva trail and

Piva village. And the Americans were already bringing in new troops. Elements of the U.S. Army 148th Infantry arrived on November 8. The Twenty-first Marines came on November 11. The army's 129th Infantry began coming on November 13.

In order to build the airfields, the Americans had to move the Japanese south and out of the area completely. But Colonel Hamanoue was still on the Piva trail. The marines began a cleanup attack on November 13, but it bogged down in heavy fighting with the determined Japanese. One company of marines got tangled up behind the Japanese and was lost for hours. Finally, they emerged from the jungle unhurt.

That night the commander of the Twenty-first Marines, Colonel Evàns O. Ames, came up the trail to see what was holding things up. He got the communications between artillery and infantry in shape and brought up some tanks to throw against Colonel Hamanoue. He also called for an air strike the next morning to start things going again. When the air strikes came in, there was a good deal of confusion. The marines overran the Japanese, who stuck in pockets of resistance, cut communications, and generally harried the Americans. After two days the marines attained their objective. They had been fighting a single company of Japanese.

Colonel Hamanoue knew that, as skillful as his soldiers were, he could not oppose the Americans' combination of artillery, air power, tanks, and infantry for very long with only a few hundred men. But he could make life very uncomfortable for the marines and the American soldiers. And he did.

Meanwhile, at sea and in the air the fighting was constant. The Japanese kept funnelling planes into Rabaul, and the Americans kept attacking Rabaul with aircraft from Fifth Air Force, and the carrier forces, and the Airsols group. Halsey temporarily had the use of five carriers, the *Princeton*, *Saratoga*, *Essex*, *Bunker Hill*, and *Independence*. Every day the Japanese came to attack the bridgehead and the ships around it. They bombed the transport *President* Jackson and the cruiser *Birmingham*, but neither ship sank.

American carrier planes attacked the Rabaul area, sinking the destroyer *Suzunami*, and damaging the destroyer *Naganami*, and knocking the stern off the cruiser *Agano*.

On the night of November 12, Japanese planes from Rabaul found elements of the American fleet at Bougainville and torpedoed the cruiser *Denver*. She was saved and towed back to Guadalcanal, which was now a safe zone.

By November 11, Colonel Hamanoue was still fighting on the hillside above the American invasion area, but he was growing very discouraged. He had been reinforced by elements of his regiment, so that at one point he had two thousand men, but casualties amounting to about three hundred men had eaten into that figure by 15 percent. And he could see no bettering of the situation in sight. He knew that the Americans were bringing in more and more troops, but the number of troops did not bother the colonel as much as the artillery and air power that the enemy was able to muster, but he was not. In fact, the Americans now had thirty-four thousand men on the island in this one area, as well as artillery that ranged from mortars to 75-mm guns, to 105-mm howitzer and 155-mm guns. Facing this enormous firepower, Colonel Hamanoue, with a few 75-mm pieces, was doing a remarkable job. By holding the trail system in bondage as he was doing, he was preventing the Americans from building their airfields. The only access to the front against the Japanese was along the Piva trail. A man wounded at the front might require the help of a whole squad to get back to the hospital, and every machine gun, every round of ammunition, every field gun, had to be horsed over the winding trail.

Every day and every night the Japanese airmen from Rabaul were out and over Bougainville, fighting the Allied aircraft, seeking out the Allied ships for attack. On November 16 the fifth convoy to supply the Bougainville bridgehead moved toward Cape Torokina. The Japanese airmen were alert. That night a torpedo plane put a "fish" into the destroyer transport *McKean*. It set off depth charges in the magazine and the resulting fireworks prompted many marines to jump overboard, where they fell into pools of burning oil and were killed or injured. The ship moved out of the oil and then was abandoned. Most of the crew and passengers were saved before she sank, but fifty-two marines were lost and sixty-four crewmen from the *McKean*.

The Japanese claims were now more elaborate and more unreliable than ever. That day they sank only the *McKean*, but Imperial Headquarters solemnly reported, as having been sunk, one large carrier, two medium-sized carriers, three cruisers, and one warship, three transports, and one destroyer, plus one transport grounded.

Given this misinformation, it was hard to see how army and navy planners could make any plans at all. One thing was certain. Either the Americans had an enormous number of warships or there was something wrong with the reporting. During the RO Operation the Japanese air force claimed to have destroyed about three times as many Allied warships as existed in the whole of the South Pacific.

On land the fighting continued as Colonel Hamanoue conducted a brilliant rearguard action. The marines kept applying the pressure, bringing up fresh troops to reinforce those on the trails. Hamanoue had no fresh troops, and by November 23 he had been forced back south along the east-west trail. The Japanese had lost their observation post on Empress Augusta Bay. The marines were building the pressure on the Numa Numa trail, and on November 23 they brought up seven battalions of artillery to cover the Japanese area with 75-mm, 105-mm, and 155-mm shells.

November 24 was the day set by the marines for a new attack. At H hour, when the marine infantry began its advance, so heavy had been the artillery barrage that they met no live Japanese. The whole area had been saturated with artillery fire and the living Japanese had vanished, retreated. The marines moved five hundred yards before they met any opposition at all, and supported by their artillery, they took their objectives that day.

On November 25 at a place called Grenade Hill, about seventy Japanese delayed the advance for a whole day. But Colonel Hamanoue knew that the end was coming, so that night the Japanese moved out. The next day the marines achieved their objective.

That was the end of the advance. The Americans had what they wanted, control of the heights above their beachhead and the site that would be the Piva bomber airfield.

Colonel Hamanoue took his battered twenty-third Infantry back down south. In the future, Japanese efforts here would be confined to raids, which would always be troublesome to the Allies but never fatal to the main program: the reduction of Rabaul by bombing. The symbol of success was the landing of the first American fighter plane on the airstrip that had been built by the Seabees down by the beach while the marines were fighting their way along the ridge trails.

There would be more fighting, including a very foolish, badly planned, and failed fight by the First Marine Parchute Battalion. On November 29 the battalion was sent to land on a beach to the south, along with a part of the Third Marine Raider Battalion. The planning was so bad that the troops were landed on Koiari beach, not knowing that it was a Japanese camp. The troops were greeted as they came out of their small boats by a Japanese officer with a samurai sword who thought they were Japanese reinforcements. Almost immediately the marines were pinned down on this beach and remained that way until they could be extricated. The rescue was a difficult job because every time the landing craft tried to approach the beach, the Japanese laid down a mortar and artillery barrage and drove them off. Meanwhile, the Japanese were attacking the marines on the beach almost incessantly.

Not until the night of November 30, after a heavy bombardment from Allied big guns at Torokina, and shelling of the Japanese by three destroyers off the beach, could the marines be rescued from the failed mission. They had suffered seventeen marines killed and ninety-five wounded. As usual they made exorbitant claims about the number of Japanese they had done away with, but the claims were not believable. The simple fact was that because of bad intelligence and bad planning the marines had been landed in the wrong place at the wrong time, in the heart of a Japanese enclave, and the mission had been a complete failure.

The Japanese continued to attack on Bougainville, mostly from the air, but as the weeks went on, it became ever more obvious that the power of the Rabaul air force was dwindling, while that of the Americans in the South and Southwest Pacific was building every day.

The Japanese sent more troops to Bougainville. In the end they numbered about eighty thousand. They did not understand the American aims, expected another landing in the north or south, and prepared themselves to fight there. But there was to be no more landing by the Americans. They had secured what they wanted at Empress Augusta Bay. It would take the Japanese several months to find out what the plan was.

A major change in the sea war occurred in the last week in November. It began because the American radio intelligence team at Pearl Harbor intercepted a message indicating a new supply mission for Buka in the southern part of Bougainville Island. The mission was to bring in material and troops as a part of the Japanese buildup to stop a new American landing. Admiral Halsey detailed Captain Arleigh Burke's Destroyer Squadron 23 to stop the mission. Burke was one of the new breed of fighting destroyer men, and that night he had five destroyers under his command. They attacked with torpedoes, blowing up the destroyers *Onami* and *Makinami* and sinking the destroyer *Yugiri* with gunfire. The destroyers *Amagiri* and *Uzuki* escaped.

There was a dramatic sequel to this sea action: General Imamura issued an order ending all efforts to reinforce Bougainville from Rabaul. It was the first fruit of the Allied policy to isolate Rabaul. And it was brought about by the skilled naval action that had finally developed in the American fleet, and by the preponderance of air power which now definitely lay with the Americans.

The Japanese effort to stop the Americans on Bougainville did continue. In December, the marines tried to clean out the whole area of the east-west trail, northward to the mountains. They encountered a company of Colonel Hamanoue's Twenty-third Infantry in a real citadel, a fortress, which the marines called "Hellzapoppin Ridge." The battle lasted six days, during which the effect of the American artillery was blunted by the deep dugouts into which the Japanese had burrowed. A combination of air strikes, mortar barrages, attack by two battalions of marines finally squeezed the Japanese out the north end of the position, and the survivors as usual disappeared into the jungle. The marines had suffered twelve men killed and twenty-three wounded. They counted about fifty Japanese bodies.

The Japanese continued to man positions not far from the American perimeter, but they could do no more than that in December. Meanwhile the American airfields around Rabaul were proliferating. On December 10 Marine squadron VMF 216 began operations from the Torokina field. Two army squadrons began operating from airfields on Stirling Island in the Treasury group. Three heavy bombardment squadrons were working out of Munda. The two upper airstrips at Bougainville were almost ready.

At the end of December the marines were replaced by army troops. The assault phase of the Bougainville operation was over. The army would garrison the island, but that did not mean they would not have to fight. Major General John R. Hodge, commander of the American Division, expected Japanese attacks.

But the Japanese did not attack. They did not seem to know what was happening. Then, at the end of December a landing party hit Green Island northwest of Buka, 167 miles west of Rabaul. Three weeks later Halsey landed 6000 troops there. They wiped out the small Japanese garrison, and the Americans began building an airstrip there.

Suddenly General Imamura and General Hyukatake, commander of the Seventeenth Army now on Bougainville, understood the American plan. The enemy was going to surround Rabaul with airfields and then attack. So they decided that the time had come to wipe out the American enclave in Empress Augusta Bay. On March 7, General Hyukatake began an attack. It was to move in three prongs against the American positions high on the side of the mountain, capture the airfield sites, and then drive down and force the Americans into the sea off Cape Torokona.

The three columns moved, and the battle raged for three weeks of deadly fighting, in which the Japanese and Americans surpassed themselves. The U.S. army held as valiantly as the marines had ever done, and the result was that the Japanese advance failed. The Japanese employed 9500 shock troops of three crack Japanese regiments, but they could not conquer the Americal Division, and finally retired south, exhausted. The Americans had been on the defensive, and when they had given ground, they had done so stubbornly. They had suffered only about a thousand casualties, 263 of them deaths. The Japanese, on the other hand had suffered seven thousand casualties, three thousand of them deaths. Once again, as with the marines, it had been the American artillery that made the big difference—the artillery and the air strikes called down by the infantry.

On March 20 Admiral Halsey tightened the noose around Rabaul a little more by sending an occupation force to little Emirau Island, seventy-five miles northwest of Kavieng. Along with the MacArthur occupation of Cape Gloucester on New Britain Island, this completed the encirclement of Rabaul with American air base sites.

By this time the Allied plan was understood in Tokyo and at Rabaul. In February the American fleet had attacked Truk, and Admiral Koga had removed the headquarters of the Combined Fleet to the Palau Island. So now Truk was nothing and Rabaul was encircled. About a hundred thousand Japanese soldiers and sailors were within the circle and another hundred thousand were left outside the new Japanese defense perimeter, languishing on tropical islands where they were supplied, if at all, only by the rare ship, and mostly by submarine. That is how it would be for the rest of the war. For the Pacific war in that spring of 1944 had moved to the Central Pacific. The Gilbert Islands had been taken in November, 1943. The Marshall islands would soon be attacked, and then, in the summer, the Marianas, which meant the breach of the line of the Japanese Inner Empire. Then the battle would move on to the Philippines.*

After Guadalcanal, and certainly after the fierce battle for Munda, the issue in the Pacific was no longer in doubt. American productivity was so great that no amount of valor or sacrifice could overcome it. What the world was to see after the beginning of 1944 was the spectacle of brave men throwing away their lives uselessly in an attempt to buy time for a solution to the war that the Japanese military and political leaders had no chance of achieving.

*For the story of the invasion of the Gilberts, see Volume 5 of this series. For the Marshalls and Marianas, see Volume 6. For MacArthur's return to the Philiippines, see Volume 8.

Bougainville, the bastion of the Solomons in the South Pacific, did not surrender until the end of the war, but as of the spring of 1944, the South Pacific campaign was really finished.

NOTES

1 The First Disaster

The basic sources for the story of Vice Admiral Frank Jack Fletcher's desertion of the first Marine Division on Guadalcanal are Admiral Morison's official naval history and Admiral Dyer's biography of Admiral Richmond Kelly Turner. The Japanese version of the Battle of Savo Island comes from the Japanese official war history.

2 After the Nightmare

The story of Colonel Goettge comes from the official reports of the Marine first Division on Guadalcanal, and from General Griffith's *Battle for Guadalcanal*. The account of the deliberations of Tojo in Tokyo is from the Japanese official war history. The remarks about "marine" and the Japanese army's ignorance on the subject is from the Ugaki diary. The story of Colonel Ichiki is from the official Japanese war history.

3 Makin Diversion

The story of the Makin raid is from my own *Raider Battalion*, (Pinnacle: 1981). My original source was a paper in the U.S. Naval Academy Library at Annapolis, written by a midshipman who had studied the records of the raid.

4 A Question of Misinformation

The material about Colonel Ichiki's detachment is from General Griffith's book and from the Japanese official history. Additional material about the Tenaru River battle comes from the Marine Corps history of Guadalcanal operations. Admiral Yamamoto's moves are chronicled in the war diary of Matome Ugaki, who was then Yamamoto's chief of staff. The story of Admiral Fletcher's encounter with the enemy is from the action reports of the task force. The material about the Kawaguchi brigade is from the Japanese war history. The story of the first Marine Raider Battalion is from the Marine Corps record and the Griffith book. The remarks about Admiral Turner's reactions are from Dyer's biography of Admiral Turner.

5 Edson's Ridge
The story of Edson's Ridge is from Richard Tregaskis's *Guadalcanal Diary*, Griffith's book, the official marine history, and the official Japanese history.

6 Crisis
The story of the eleventh Air Fleet's operations is from some translations I made from *Rabauru*, a book written in 1978 by survivors about the operations of that fleet in this period. The material about Lieutenant Colonel Tsuji is from the Ugaki diary. Tsuji was one of the fascinating characters of the Japanese army, a man of enormous strength of character who exerted influence far surpassing his rank. Men like Admiral Yamamoto listened when Tsuji spoke. And, as noted in this and other volumes of this series, Tsuji had a wide influence over events: he was partly responsible for Tojo's cashiering of General Yamashita after Yamashita's brilliant victory in Malaya, and also for the forced retirement of General Homma from the Philippines for "softness." The stories about the naval encounters are from the U.S. Naval records and the Japanese war history. The story of the Nimitz-Ghormley confrontation is from my own book, *How They Won The War in The Pacific*, and is based on Nimitz's correspondence and records.

7 Henderson
The story of Admiral Yamamoto's meetings is from the Ugaki diary. The story of Ghormley's activity is from the Dyer book and from the U.S. South Pacific operations reports. Halsey's reaction to his new assignment is recorded in the Bryan book. The story of the Japanese movements on Guadalcanal is from the official Japanese war history.

8 Attack and Attack
The story of Colonel Furumiya and his regiment and the "capture" of Henderson Field is from the Ugaki diary and from the official Japanese war history, from which I took the translations. General Griffith's book tells part of the story, but he misidenti-

fies Colonel Furumiya, calling him Ishimiya. (The Chinese characters for ishi-stone and furu-old are similar.) To me, the most interesting note about the battle was the revelation that the "Banzai attack" staged by the Japanese was not at the instigation of their leaders, but the result of hysteria.

9 The Battle of the Santa Cruz Islands

The fact that the army had failed again brought Admiral Yamamoto to the point of despair, for it did not seem to make much difference how many victories he won at sea, the army was negating them by its failure to deploy enough men on Guadalcanal to take the island back. Admiral Nagumo's actions and attitudes are indicated in the Ugaki diary. My own observations about Nagumo are colored by my study of Yamamoto's carer for my biography of the admiral and the discovery that Yamamoto and Nagumo were old adversaries from the days of the Fleet Faction vs. the Treaty Faction during the 1930s, when Admiral Yamamoto espoused cooperation with the Western powers and Admiral Nagumo belonged to the extreme nationalist faction of the navy.

The story of the battle of the Santa Cruz islands is from Morison, from the Japanese official naval history, and from a long interview I had with Admiral Kinkaid in the 1960s.

10 The Balance at Sea

The notes about Hirohito and Yamamoto come from materials for my biographies of both men. Admiral Turner's reactions come from the Dyer book. The story of the Battle of Guadalcanal is from the Morison history and from the official Japanese history. The most important development of this battle was the proof that the Americans now controlled the air over Guadalcanal and that all Yamamoto's efforts to reinforce the army on Guadalcanal would fail unless he could get the resources to take what the Japanese called "mastery of the air." Had the army authorities recognized the problem, they could have made hundreds of army planes available, but communications between army and navy were still virtually nonexistent, and the army did nothing to help at this critical juncture, when it had 25,000 men on Guadalcanal.

11 The Battleships

The story of the battleships is from Morison and from the Japanese official history.

12 For the Moment, a Draw . . .

As the Ugaki diary and the official Japanese war history indicate, in mid-November 1942 the army suddenly saw that the situation on Guadalcanal was serious, although they did not realize how serious. They promised cooperation with the navy, and this meant air cooperation for the most part. From the American point of view, the Guadalcanal campaign had settled down to a slugfest the U.S. Army is usually better at this than the U.S. Marine Corps, but this was not readily apparent in the fall of 1942, because the army troops who came to Guadalcanal were not very well trained. The new Tanaka method of supplying Guadalcanal was an indication of the navy's growing desperation of the Japanese navy.

13 The Battle of Tassafaronga

As is shown by the outcome of the Battle of Tassafaronga, the Japanese could win all the battles at sea and still lose the campaign. They did it again here, but did not solve the problem of supplying the troops on the island. Tassafaronga simply confirmed Admiral Yamamoto's distrust of Admiral Tanaka's effectiveness in the supply run, which was ultimately unfair of Yamamoto. Soon Tanaka would disappear from the scene, with scarcely word, not even in the Ugaki diary.

14 The End on Guadalcanal

General Griffith tells the story of the changeover from marine to army command. So does the official U.S. Army history and Morison. The account of the visits of army and navy leaders to the Imperial Palace is from materials for my book, *Hirohito*. The account of Admiral Giffen's fights is from Morison's history. The account of the Japanese evacuation of Guadalcanal is from the official war history.

15 The Submarines

The accounts of the submarines and naval activity in the South and Southwest Pacific comes from official American records. Part of the material comes from correspondence with Admiral Christie, part from an interview with Rear Admiral Fife.

16 "Stop the Enemy . . . "

The story about Hirohito and the war comes from records of Tojo's regime, and is repeated in several biographies of Tojo published in Japan. The story of the invasion of the Russells is from Morison's history.

17 The Struggle for Air Power

The American buildup in the Solomons is described by Morison. The story of the I-Operation comes from material I gathered for my biography of Admiral Yamamoto, the sources are indicated in that bibliography. The remarks about Admiral Draemel and other figures in the transition period from peace to war are taken from my observations after interviewing such men as Admiral Draemel, Admiral Fitch, and Admiral Harry Hill.

18 New Georgia

The death of Yamamoto comes from descriptions in my biography of Yamamoto and from Burke Davis's *Get Yamamoto*. Halsey's Munda plans are detailed in the operations reports and war diary of the South Pacific command and in Morison's history. Admiral Turner's activities are chronicled in the Dyer biography. The story of the naval campaign around New Georgia is told from the Japanese point of view in Hara's *Japanese Destroyer Captain*. Gregory Boyington's book *Baa Baa Black Sheep*, while in no way official, has some interesting sidelights on the campaign. The story of General Sasaki's efforts is from the Japanese official war history.

19 Munda

The story of the battle for Munda comes from the marine history, the Japanese official history, and Morison's history.

20 Change in Strategy

The discussion of the Japanese change in strategy comes from materials on General Tojo, from the official Japanese war history, and from Morison's history. The accounts of the activities of Arleigh Burke come from a number of interviews with Admiral Burke I conducted in the 1970s; my observations about the American destroyers also come from those conversations. The island bypass campaign is credited to everyone from General MacArthur to Admiral Halsey, but the fact seems to be that it was first suggested in the Joint Chiefs of Staff, and that after that everyone saw it as an obvious method of dealing with the problem of attenuated campaigns, given the fact that American naval and air strength was increasing all the time, while that of the Japanese was waning. The accounts of the battle at sea are from Morison and from the Japanese official war history.

21 Bougainville Assault

The story of the attack on Bougainville is from Morison's history, the official Japanese history, and the marine history.

22 Admiral Omori Attacks

The story of naval actions around Bougainville comes from the official Japanese war history and from Morison. The notes about Admiral Sherman's operations are from materials collected for my book *Carrier Wars*, (McGraw Hill: 1989).

23 The Fight for Bougainville

The story of Colonel Hamanoue comes from the Japanese official war history. The story of the marines' fight for the mountain trails is from the official marine history. The story of the gaffe in the landing of the marine parachutists and Raiders at Koiari beach is from Morison and from the marine history. The notes about the attitude of General John R. Hodge come from my interviews with General Hodge after the war.

BIBLIOGRAPHY

Documents

War Diary Comsopac, 1943-4

Cincpac Fleet Reports, Solomons

Occupation of Bougainville and Supporting Operations

Joint Chiefs of Staff History, Occupation of New Georgia and Vella Lavella

Cincpac War Diary

Cincpac Gray Book

Nimitz-Halsey correspondence

King-Nimitz Conferences

All of the above are in the Operational Archives of the United States Navy in the Naval History Center, Washington Navy Yard.

Books

Agawa, Hiroyuki. *The Reluctant Admiral: Yamamoto and the Imperial Navy*. Tokyo: Kodansha International, 1979.

Boei cho Kenshujo Senshishitsu Senshi Sosho (The Japanese Defense Agency's Official History of the Pacific War). Sixvolumes on the South Pacific. Tokyo: Japanese Defense Agency, 1950-1970.

Boyington, Gregory. *Baa Baa Black Sheep*. New York: G. P. Putnam's Sons, 1958.

Bryan, J. and W. F. Halsey. *Admiral Halsey's Story*. New York: Da Capo Press, 1976.

Davis, Burke. *Get Yamamoto*. New York: Random House, 1970.

Dyer, George C. *The Amphibians Came to Conquer: A Biography of Admiral Richmond Kelly Turner*. Two vols. Washington: U.S. Government Printing Office, undated.

Griffith, Samuel B., II. *The Battle for Guadalcanal*. Philadelphia: J. B. Lippincott, 1963.

Hara Tameichi. *Japanese Destroyer Captain*. New York: Ballantine Books, 1961.

Hayashi, Saburo, with Alvin D. Koontz. *Kogun: The Japanese Army in the Pacific War*. Washington: The Marine Corps Association, 1959.

Hess, W. N. *Pacific Sweep*. Garden City, N.Y.: Doubleday and Co., 1974.

Hoshina, Zenshiro, et al. *Dai Hei Yo Senso Hishi (The Secret History of the Pacific War)*. Tokyo: Nihon koku Bokyo Sha, 1987.

Matsushima, Keizo. *Yamamoto Isoroku*. Tokyo: Tonaji Shuppansha, 1953.

Morison, Samuel Eliot. *History of United States Naval Operations in World War II*. Vol. 5, *Guadalcanal*, Vol. II, *Breaking the Bismarcks Barrier*. Boston: Little Brown, 1949.

Nomura, Minoru. *Rekishi no naka no nihonklkaigun, (The Inside History of the Japanese Navy)*. Tokyo: Genshobo, 1970.

Ochi, Harukai. *Gadarukanaru*. Tokyo: Tosho shuppangaisha, 1975.

Rentz, John N. *Bougainville and the Northern Solomons*. Washington: Historical Section, U.S. Marine Corps, 1948.

Rentz, John N. *Marines in the Central Solomons*. Washington: Historical Section, U.S. Marine Corps, 1962.

Sorimachi, Eiichi, Ningen. *Yamamoto Isoroku: Gensai no Shogai*. Tokyo: Hikawado, 1970.

Tregaskis, Richard. *Guadalcanal Diary*. New York: Random House, 1943.

Ugaki, Matome. *Dai Toa Senso Hiki (War Diary)*. Tokyo: Gensho Moshi, 1970.

INDEX

WORLD WAR II
Edwin P. Hoyt

STORM OVER THE GILBERTS: 63651-4/$3.50 US/$4.50 Can
War in the Central Pacific: 1943
The dramatic reconstruction of the bloody battle over the Japanese-held Gilbert Islands.

CLOSING THE CIRCLE: 67983-8/$3.50 US/$4.95 Can
War in the Pacific: 1945
A behind-the-scenes look at the military and political moves drawn from official American and Japanese sources.

McCAMPBELL'S HEROES   68841-7/$3.95 US/$5.75 Can
A stirring account of the daring fighter pilots, led by Captain David McCampbell, of Air Group Fifteen.

LEYTE GULF   75408-8/$3.50 US/$4.50 Can
The Death of the Princeton
The true story of a bomb-torn American aircraft carrier fighting a courageous battle for survival!

WAR IN THE PACIFIC: SOUTH PACIFIC   76158-0/$4.50 US/$5.50 Can

WAR IN THE PACIFIC: TRIUMPH OF JAPAN
         75792-3/$4.50 US/$5.50 Can

WAR IN THE PACIFIC: STIRRINGS   75793-1/$3.95 US/$4.95 Can

THE JUNGLES OF NEW GUINEA   75750-8/$4.95 US/$5.95 Can

Buy these books at your local bookstore or use this coupon for ordering:
....

Mail to: Avon Books, Dept BP, Box 767, Rte 2, Dresden, TN 38225
Please send me the book(s) I have checked above.
☐ My check or money order—no cash or CODs please—for $_____ is enclosed
(please add $1.00 to cover postage and handling for each book ordered to a maximum of
three dollars—Canadian residents add 7% GST).
☐ Charge my VISA/MC Acct#_____Exp Date_____
Phone No_____ I am ordering a minimum of two books (please add
postage and handling charge of $2.00 plus 50 cents per title after the first two books to a
maximum of six dollars—Canadian residents add 7% GST). For faster service, call 1-800-
762-0779. Residents of Tennessee, please call 1-800-633-1607. Prices and numbers are
subject to change without notice. Please allow six to eight weeks for delivery.

Name_____

Address _____

City_____ State/Zip _____

HOY 0591

THE GREAT BATTLES OF WW II
by the award-winning
THEODORE TAYLOR

THE BATTLE OFF MIDWAY ISLAND
78790-3/
$3.95 US/$4.95 Can

Recounts the savage fight on the sea and in the air that changed the course of the war in the Pacific.

H.M.S. HOOD VS. BISMARCK:
THE BATTLESHIP BATTLE
81174-X/
$3.95 US/$4.95 Can

A dramatic portrayal of the legendary battles between H.M.S. *Hood* and Germany's awesome masterpiece of naval construction, the *Bismarck*

BATTLE IN THE ENGLISH CHANNEL
85225-X/
$3.50 US/$4.25 Can

Replay the daring escape in December 1941 taken by Hitler's ships out of Brest—up the English Channel through mine-infested waters…right under the nose of the British.

ROCKET ISLAND
89674-5/
$3.50 US/$4.25 Can

A riveting account of Nazi Germany's development and implementation of the devastating V-1 and V-2 rockets against Britain.

Buy these books at your local bookstore or use this coupon for ordering:

Mail to: Avon Books, Dept BP, Box 767, Rte 2, Dresden, TN 38225
Please send me the book(s) I have checked above.
☐ My check or money order—no cash or CODs please—for $_____ is enclosed
(please add $1.00 to cover postage and handling for each book ordered to a maximum of
three dollars—Canadian residents add 7% GST).
☐ Charge my VISA/MC Acct# _____ Exp Date _____
Phone No _____ I am ordering a minimum of two books (please add
postage and handling charge of $2.00 plus 50 cents per title after the first two books to a
maximum of six dollars—Canadian residents add 7% GST). For faster service, call 1-800-
762-0779. Residents of Tennessee, please call 1-800-633-1607. Prices and numbers are
subject to change without notice. Please allow six to eight weeks for delivery.

Name_____

Address _____

City _____ State/Zip _____

TT 0391